C'EST POUR MON CRAPAUD

and Other Useful French Phrases

JEAN-LOUP CHIFLET

Illustrations by Christine Géricot

MICHAEL O'MARA BOOKS LIMITED

First published in Great Britain in 1996 by
Michael O'Mara Books Limited
9 Lion Yard
Tremadoc Road
London SW4 7NQ

First published in France in 1993 by Éditions Payot &
Rivages

A CIP catalogue record for this book is available from the
British Library

The right of Jean-Loup Chiflet to be identified as the
author of this work had been asserted by him in accordance
with the Copyright, Designs and Patents Act, 1988.

ISBN 1-85479-623-2

Printed and bound in Great Britain by
Cox & Wyman Ltd, Reading, Berkshire

INTRODUCTION

You've always wanted one? You could never find it?

Here it is!

At last the world's first really essential French-English phrase book. Easy-to-use French for situations in which YOU often find yourself.

You get beaten up in the police station? You bump into the Pope at the Vatican? The butcher threatens to use you as steak? Your analyst reaches for his scissors? The stuffing is coming out of your parrot? The flagellants are late at the convent? No problem. Just reach for this little book – you're bound to find the *mot juste*.

And not only that. The book also provides a series of illustrated plates to help you acquaint yourself with essential everyday vocabulary – the working parts of a sheep, the inside of a windmill, and the intimated details of an oyster. Think what a wow you are going to be at Parisian parties! They'll be waiting for you on the platform as soon as you step off the Eurostar ready to whisk you off to glittering candlelit dinners! 'Oh Brian, do remind us of the intimate mechanism of the metronome!' 'What exactly was the tarsus of the hen?' You're going to be the belle of the ball (especially if you wear a dress).

This, then – in every sense of the word – is the phrase book to end all phrase books …

Just a minute! Here I am, driving through the French Alps in my blue fork-lift truck when I pull into a lay-by and bump into an attractive nun knitting pullovers for the Save the Goat foundation … I only have to slip this precious little book out of my back pocket and …

Robert est votre oncle!

Bon Voyage!

Jean-Loup Chiflet 1996

SITUATION FRENCH

AU COMMISSARIAT DE POLICE
AT THE POLICE STATION

- **Où puis-je laver mes petites menottes ?**

  Could I please go and wash my little handcuffs ?

- **Madame la commissaire, je vous trouve très belle, j'aimerais vous faire une déclaration ?**

  (Speaking to the Female Police Chief) : You're very beautiful. May I make my declaration ?

- **Auriez-vous l'obligeance de détacher ce radiateur de mes poignets ?**

  Would you be so kind as to untie the radiator from my wrists ?

- **Rendez-moi mes lacets car je vais prendre froid aux pieds avec ces courants d'air.**

  Please give me back my shoelaces or my feet will get cold from these drafts.

- **Ça avait la couleur de l'alcool, ça ressemblait à de l'alcool, mais vous avez raison monsieur l'agent, je crois que c'était vraiment de l'alcool.**

  It was the same colour as alcohol and it looked just like alcohol. You know, I think you're right, Officer, it really was alcohol.

VOCABULARY

Bavure = Unfortunate mistake	**Viol** = Rape
Matraque = Truncheon	**Ceinturon** = Belt
Contravention = Fine	**Violon** = Prison
Immigré = Immigrant	**Visière** = Peak
Patibulaire = Sinister	**Avocat** = Lawyer
Machine à écrire = Typewriter	**Innocent** = Innocent

CHEZ UN MILLIARDAIRE
AT A BILLIONAIRE'S HOUSE

- **Qui a pris le Rembrandt qui était dans la salle de bains ?**

  Who took the Rembrandt that was in the bathroom ?

- **Les orchidées de la niche du chien sont fanées.**

  The orchids in the doghouse have wilted.

- **Quelle Liz a téléphoné, Taylor ou la Reine ?**

  Which Liz was that on the telephone, Taylor or the Queen ?

- **Je trouve que les enfants ne devraient pas griffonner sur les Picasso. Ça fait désordre.**

  I don't think the children should scribble on the Picassos. It looks so sloppy.

- **Si l'hélicoptère est en panne, comment vais-je faire pour aller chercher le pain ?**

  How will I get to the bakery if the helicopter isn't working ?

VOCABULARY

Or = Gold

Pouvoir = Power

Yacht = Yacht

Spéculation = Speculation

Vison = Mink

Maître d'hôtel = Butler

Truffe = Truffle

Esturgeon = Sturgeon

Bourse = Stock Exchange

Magot = Pile

Luxe = Luxury

Plaqué or = Gold plate

JE VOYAGE AU JAPON
MY TRIP TO JAPAN

- **Ne mets pas tes genoux sur la table.**

  Don't put your knees on the table !

- **A quelle heure rentre le kamikaze ?**

  What time is the kamikaze coming home ?

- **Pour le petit déjeuner j'avais dit « café complet » et non pas « riz complet » !**

  I ordered a continental breakfast with coffee, not with rice !

- **Madame la geisha, si vous voulez courir pour attraper votre train, vous feriez mieux de mettre un jogging.**

  If you have to run to catch your train, you'd be better off wearing sweat pants... even if you are a Geisha.

- **Mais non, monsieur le sumo, ce n'est pas parce que vous êtes anorexique qu'il faut vous faire hara-kiri.**

  Just because you're a sumo wrestler doesn't mean you have to commit hara-kiri for being anorexic.

VOCABULARY

Yeux bridés = Slanting eyes

Poisson cru = Raw fish

Empereur = Emperor

Courbette = Low bow

Bombe atomique = Nuclear bomb

Tremblement de terre = Earthquake

Rizière = Ricefield

Yamaha = Yamaha

Cerf-volant = Kite

Honda = Honda

Temple = Temple

Jaune = Yellow

CHEZ LE PSYCHANALYSTE
AT THE ANALYST'S

- **Je jouais effectivement au football au stade municipal, mais je n'ai jamais été ni au stade oral ni au stade anal.**

  I used to act in plays on the community theatre stage, but I never got to the oral or anal stage.

- **Si j'avais su qu'il fallait que je me couche sur ce divan j'aurais apporté mon pyjama et mon nounours.**

  If I had known I was going to lie down on this couch, I would have brought my teddy bear and pyjamas.

- **Je crois que vous faites erreur. Ma mère n'était pas castratrice, mais cantatrice.**

  I think you're misunderstood. I said my mother practised emancipation, not emasculation.

- **Lorsque vous décroisez vos jambes, madame la psychothérapeute, je sens le réservoir de ma libido se destructurer en vue d'un transfert analysant analysé.**

(Speaking to a female therapist) : When you uncross your legs, I feel my libido coming undone and getting geared for an analyst-analysand transfer.

VOCABULARY

Schizophrénie = Schizophrenia	**Phallique** = Phallic
Narcissique = Narcissistic	**Pulsion** = Drive
Névrotique = Neurotic	**Phobique** = Phobic
Borderline = Borderline	**Pénis** = Penis
Projection = Projection	**Fantasme** = Fantasy
Régression = Regression	**Œdipe** = Œdipus

A L'ACADÉMIE FRANÇAISE
AT THE FRENCH ACADEMY

- **Je vous trouve très vert pour votre âge.**

  You do seem quite spry for your age.

- **Où doit-on s'adresser pour participer au goûter costumé du jeudi après-midi ?**

  Where is the Thursday afternoon costume tea party being held ?

- **J'aimerais visiter la salle de musculation.**

  I'd like to see the work-out room.

- **Où se trouvent les toilettes pour femmes ?**

  Where is the ladies' room ?

- **Dès que vous aurez fini votre sieste, pourrez-vous terminer la lettre B ?**

  As soon as your nap is over, could you finish the letter B ?

VOCABULARY

Épeler = To spell

Pluriel = Plural

Pléonasme = Pleonasm

Consonne = Consonant

Épithète = Epithet

Mot = Word

Glossaire = Glossary

Alphabet = Alphabet

Voyelle = Vowel

Verbe = Verb

Complément = Complement

Singulier = Singular

CHEZ LE TAXIDERMISTE
AT THE TAXIDERMIST'S

● **J'aimerais que vous consolidiez l'andouiller de mon wapiti, car j'ai huit enfants et j'aimerais qu'ils puissent accrocher leurs manteaux.**

I'd like you to reinforce my wapiti antlers so that my eight children can hang up their overcoats on them.

● **Mon orang-outan devait être prêt à 15 h. Que se passe-t-il ?**

What's going on ? My orangutang was supposed to be ready by 3.

● **Pour ma pieuvre, j'aimerais que vous me fassiez un prix : le huitième tentacule gratuit.**

Could you give me a deal on that octopus ? How about the eighth tentacle for free ?

- **Auriez-vous un joli diplodocus, mais plutôt nain, car c'est pour un milieu de table ?**

  I'm looking for an attractive diplodocus, but it has to be a miniature because it's for a centre-piece.

- **Pouvez-vous réparer mon serpent à sonnette ? Il ne fonctionne plus.**

  Could you repair my rattlesnake, please ? It doesn't work any more.

VOCABULARY

Hareng = Herring

Chinchilla = Chinchilla

Tapir = Tapir

Pou = Louse

Putois = Polecat

Lamproie = Lamprey

Chat-huant = Screech owl

Mangouste = Mongoose

Cachalot = Sperm whale

Orignal = Moose

Sangsue = Leech

Silure = Silurid

AU VATICAN
AT THE VATICAN

● **Je vois que vous avez fait repeindre les plafonds, c'est du Pope art ?**

  I see you've had the ceiling repainted. Is that called Pope Art ?

● **J'aime bien votre chapeau, il est rigolo. Où l'avez-vous acheté ?**

  I really like your hat. It's so funny. Where did you get it ?

● **Je connais une trattoria dans le coin qui fait d'excellentes pâtes au basilic.**

  I know a trattoria in the area that serves great angel hair pasta.

● **j'ai vu *Rocky I, Rocky II*, mais je n'ai pas vu Vatican I ni Vatican II.**

  I've seen Rocky I and II, but I haven't seen Vatican I or Vatican II.

- **Où puis-je acheter du savon ? C'est pour offrir au pape pour qu'il me fasse une bulle.**

  Quick ! I need to find a cape. The pope is sending me a bull.

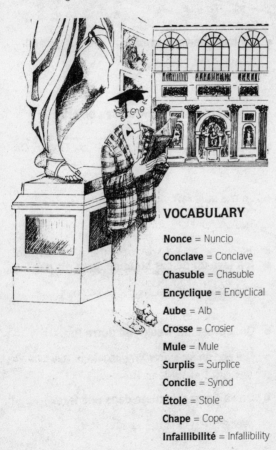

VOCABULARY

Nonce = Nuncio

Conclave = Conclave

Chasuble = Chasuble

Encyclique = Encyclical

Aube = Alb

Crosse = Crosier

Mule = Mule

Surplis = Surplice

Concile = Synod

Étole = Stole

Chape = Cope

Infaillibilité = Infallibility

LES ADOS
THE TEENAGERS

- **Tu hallucines ou quoi ?**

  Are you nuts or what ?

- **J'ai un plan d'acier avec une belette.**

  I met this chick and I'm sure it's going to work with her.

- **Je me suis fait virer du bahut.**

  I've been kicked out of school.

- **Il a levé un de ces boudins, je te dis pas !**

  You should see the dog he picked up !

- **On a passé un week-end outre fun.**

  We had an awesome time this weekend.

- **On va taper l'incruste dans une fête.**

  We're going to crash a party.

- **Pour les examens, il a le cul bordé de nouilles.**

  He's always such a lucky devil when it comes to exams.

VOCABULARY

Erreur humaine = Creep

Prise de tête = Real pain

Lézard = Problem

Enflure = Creep

Galère = Bore

Sapé = Dressed

Zoner = To wander around

Caisse = Car

Pétard = Joint

La honte = Shame

Trop = Too much

Tronche de cake = Jerk

DANS UN SOUS-MARIN
IN A SUBMARINE

● **Auriez-vous un masque et un tuba, car j'aimerais aller me promener sur le pont ?**

Have you got a mask and snorkel to lend me ?
I'd like to go for a walk up on the bridge.

● **Je n'arrive pas à ouvrir les fenêtres.**

I can't get these windows open.

● **Les essuie-glaces du périscope doivent être en panne car je ne vois plus rien.**

I can't see a thing. The periscope's windscreen wipers must be broken.

- **Mon commandant, j'ai amené le pavillon mais je le trouve très humide.**

  I raised the flag, Captain, but it's rather wet.

- **Avec un peu plus de vent nous irions probablement plus vite.**

  We could probably go faster if the wind were blowing stronger.

VOCABULARY

Hélice = Propeller

Sas d'accès arrière = Air lock

Chaudière = Boiler

Kiosque = Conning tower

Barre de plongée = Starboard diving plane

Gouvernail de plongée avant = Port sail plane

Chambre des machines = Engine room

Tube lance-missiles = Missile tube

Couchette = Bunk

Réacteur = Reactor

Torpille = Torpedo

Missile = Missile

AU RESTAURANT CHINOIS
AT A CHINESE RESTAURANT

- **Auriez-vous un peu de pain pour le fromage ?**

  Could I please have some bread to go with the cheese ?

- **Bonjour Mr Ping, n'auriez-vous pas vu mon chat car il a disparu près de chez vous ?**

  Hello ! Mr. Ping. Have you seen my cat ? It got lost near here.

- **Votre canard siamois est très bon mais je lui trouve un arrière-goût de gouttière.**

  Your Siamese duck is delicious but it has a strange aftertaste... rather like alley food.

- **J'aurais préféré des rognons de veau et du gratin dauphinois.**

  I would have prefered veal kidneys and scalloped potatoes.

- **Cette soupe chinoise paraît excellente mais j'éprouve une certaine difficulté à l'apprécier avec des baguettes.**

This Chinese soup smells delicious, but I could sure use a spoon instead of chopsticks.

VOCABULARY

Canard laqué = Peking duck

Thé = Tea

Soupe = Soup

Cure-dent = Toothpick

Vapeur = Steam

Menu = Menu

Rouleau de printemps = Spring roll

Bol = Bowl

Riz cantonais = Fried rice

Écumoire = Skimmer

Gingembre = Ginger

Wok = Wok

- **Madame l'anesthésiste, pouvez-vous me réveiller vers midi/midi et demi ?**

  Speaking to the anaesthetist : Could you please make my wake up call for around 12-12:30 ?

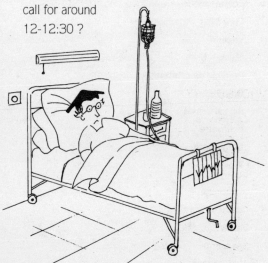

- **Enlevez votre masque, je vous ai reconnu.**

  Take off your mask. I know who you are.

- **Je ne me fais pas de mauvais sang mais je n'aime pas les transfusions.**

  I'm not too worried about it, but I don't like blood transfusions.

- **Il faut faire la queue pour passer sur le billard, et en plus, ça me donne les boules.**

  You have to queue up before being operated on. It really gives me the creeps.

- **A quelle heure doit-on changer de drain ?**

  When should we change the tubes ?

VOCABULARY

Cachet = Tablet

Prostate = Prostate

Radiographie = X-ray

Seringue = Syringe

Infirmière = Nurse

Ovaire = Ovary

Vessie = Bladder

Spéculum = Speculum

Abaisse-langue = Tongue depressor

Stimulateur cardiaque = Pacemaker

Veine cave supérieure = Superior vena cava

Oto-rhino-laryngologiste = Ear, nose and throat specialist

JE RENTRE AU COUVENT
GETTING TO A CONVENT

- **J'avais réservé une cellule avec un lit double. Passez-moi la réception.**

  I'd like to speak to the manager please, I reser-
  ved a cell with a double bed.

- **Pouvez-vous me réveiller pour matines ?**

  Could you wake me up for matins, please ?

- **A quelle heure doit-on se flageller ?**

  What time is flagellation scheduled for ?

- **Je préfère garder ma casquette car j'ai
peur de prendre froid à cause de la tonsure.**

  I'd rather keep my cap on. I'm afraid of
  catching cold with this tonsure.

- **Je croyais que les auréoles se portaient au-dessus de la tête et non sous les bras.**

  I thought halos were supposed to be worn above your head, not under your armpit.

VOCABULARY

Chasteté = Chastity

Méditation = Meditation

Novice = Novice

Foi = Faith

Cloître = Cloister

Dévotion = Devotion

Chapitre = Chapter

Extase = Ecstasy

Vœu = Vow

Parloir = Parlour

Cloche = Bell

Moine = Monk

DANS LE MÉTRO
THE UNDERGROUND

● **Dès que vous aurez fini de lire
par-dessus mon épaule, je me permettrai
de tourner la page.**

As soon as you've finished reading over my
shoulder, I'll turn the page.

- **Pardon, monsieur le contrôleur, où sont les toilettes s'il vous plaît ?**

  Excuse me, Inspector, where is the John ?

- **Je voudrais la couchette du haut.**

  I'd like the upper berth.

- **Je n'ai que quelques bagages à main mais je souhaiterais les enregistrer.**

  I've only got hand luggage, but I'd like to check it in.

- **La prochaine fois, je demanderai à l'agence de voyages de me donner des places assises dans le sens de la marche.**

  Next time I'll ask my travel agent to reserve seats facing in the direction that the train is heading.

VOCABULARY

Tourniquet = Turnstile	**Quai** = Platform
Aiguillage = Switch	**Butoir** = Bumper
Escalier mécanique = Escalator	**Rame** = Train
Barre de maintien = Side handrail	**Traverse** = Sleeper
Portes coulissantes = Sliding doors	**Voie** = Track
Motrice = Motor unit	**Siège** = Seat

DANS LES CATACOMBES
IN THE CATACOMBS

- **Comme c'est bien rangé !**

  It's so neat and tidy down here !

- **Y a quelqu'un ?**

  Is anyone home ?

- **Être ou ne pas être, là est la question.**

  To be or not to be, that's the question.

- **Échangerait radius contre cubitus.**

  Will swap a radius bone for a ulna bone.

- **Les chiens doivent être tenus en laisse.**

  Dogs must be kept on a leash.

- **N'oubliez pas le guide… à l'intérieur, s'il vous plaît.**

  Please don't leave the guide inside.

VOCABULARY

Sternum = Sternum

Omoplate = Shoulder blade

Métatarse = Metatarsal

Ilion = Ilium

Carpe = Carpus

Rotule = Knee cap

Péroné = Fibula

Clavicule = Collar bone

Crâne = Skull

Malléole = Calcaneus

Cubitus = Ulna

Sacrum = Sacrum

- **Les enfants ! Arrêtez de jouer avec ce requin et venez goûter.**

  Children ! Stop playing with that shark, come and eat your lunch.

- **Maintenant, vous allez déterrer votre grand-père car c'est lui qui a les clefs de la voiture et il faut rentrer.**

  Come on, now, it's time to go. You have to dig up grandfather. He is the one with the keys.

- **Qui a caché le monokini de grand-mère ?**

  Who hid grandmother's bikini bottoms ?

- **Crois-tu qu'il est bien utile de terminer chaque leçon de natation par un cours de bouche-à-bouche avec le maître nageur ?**

  Do you really think it's necessary to end every swimming lesson by doing mouth to mouth resuscitation with the lifeguard ?

- **J'adore cette plage parce que même quand il fait froid on peut se chauffer au mazout.**

  I love this beach. Even when it's cold you can use the oil from the slicks to get warm.

VOCABULARY

Embruns = Sea spray

Vent arrière = Rear wind

Parasol = Beach umbrella

Écume = Foam

Goémon = Wrack

Soutien-gorge = Bra

Méduse = Jellyfish

Bronzer = To get a tan

Crête = Crest

Galet = Pebble

Crevette = Prawn

Dune = Dune

A LA BANQUE
AT THE BANK

- **Que personne ne bouge ! Les mains en l'air...**

  Nobody move ! Stick'em up...

- **Ce serait pour changer des faux billets, c'est quel guichet ?**

  Excuse me, which window deals in counterfeit bills ?

- **J'ai apporté des bouteilles vides car je souhaiterais de l'argent liquide.**

  I brought empty bottles to take care of a cash flow problem...

- **Je m'appelle Spaggiari, avec 2 « g » s'il vous plaît. Suis-je à découvert ?**

  My name is Spaggiari with 2 "g's". Am I overdrawn ?

- **11-43 ? Ce n'est pas le montant du taux de prêt mais le calibre de mon revolver.**

  11-43 ? It's not the interest rate on my loan, it's the calibre of my revolver.

VOCABULARY

Spéculer = To speculate

Coffre-fort = Safe

Chèque = Cheque

Escompte = Discount

Crédit = Credit

Débiteur = Debtor

Épargne = Savings

Faillite = Bankruptcy

Créancier = Creditor

Caissier = Cashier

Action = Share

Obligation = Bond

A L'ÉGLISE
AT CHURCH

- **Où se trouve la zone non-fumeurs car je ne supporte pas l'encens ?**

  Where's the non-smoking section ? I can't bear incense.

- **Monsieur le sacristain, je n'ai qu'un franc pour la quête, pouvez-vous me rendre la monnaie ?**

  I only have one franc for the collection plate. Could you please give me back some change ?

- **Veuillez laisser, je vous prie, ce confessionnal dans l'état dans lequel vous souhaiteriez le trouver en entrant.**

  Please leave this confessional as clean as you found it upon arriving.

- **Le vin de messe nouveau est-il arrivé ?**

  Is the "vin de messe nouveau" out yet ?

- **Le prédicateur a décidé de ne pas monter en chaire car c'est une messe basse.**

  It's a low mass, so the preacher has decided not to speak from the pulpit.

VOCABULARY

Clef de voûte = Keystone

Arc-boutant = Flying buttress

Bigot = Holier-than-thou

Nef = Nave

Bénitier = Stoup

Voussure = Arch

Vicaire = Curate

Abside = Apse

Flèche = Spire

Clocher = Bell tower

Tronc = Collection box

Diocèse = Diocese

EN AVION
ON AN AIRPLANE

- **Auriez-vous l'amabilité d'ouvrir un peu votre hublot ? Je crève de chaud.**

  It's so hot in here. Would you mind opening your window a bit ?

- **Oui mon chéri, on va faire du toboggan ! Dépêche-toi et laisse ton seau et ta pelle mais prends ta bouée.**

  Yes, dear, we are going on the slide ! Hurry up now. Leave your bucket and spade, but don't forget the life belt.

- **Ces stewards ont de jolis uniformes kaki mais je n'aime pas leurs cagoules noires.**

  These stewards have such pretty khaki uniforms, but I am not very fond of their black facemasks.

- **Si le pilote continue à faire des loopings, je vais exiger de lui faire souffler dans le ballon.**

  If the pilot keeps on making these loops, I'm going to demand that he take the alcohol test.

- **OK pour atterrir dans les Andes... mais pas question de manger mon voisin, je suis végétarien.**

  It's OK by me if we land in the Andes, but I refuse to eat my neighbour. I'm a vegetarian.

VOCABULARY

Catastrophe aérienne = Plane crash

Survivant = Survivor

Détournement = Hijacking

Décollage = Takeoff

Anémomachmètre = Mach and speed indicator

Arbre turbine compresseur = Turbine compressor shaft

Chariot à bagage = Baggage cart

Trou d'air = Air pocket

Instruments de vol = Flying instruments

Boutique hors taxe = Duty free shop

Cumulo-nimbus = Cumulonimbus

Décalage horaire = Jet lag

● **Pardon, madame l'ouvreuse, pouvez-vous m'aider à sortir de la baignoire pour me mener aux lavabos ?**

(Speaking to the usherette) : Excuse me, Miss, can you help me get out of the stalls and show me the way to the conveniences ?

● **A quelle heure se termine la *Symphonie inachevée* ?**

What time does the *Unfinished Symphony* end ?

- **Le chanteur fait tellement de canards qu'il devrait se réfugier au poulailler.**

  That singer has hit too many false notes. Send him to the peanut gallery !

- **Si c'était pour danser la *Carmagnole*, c'était pas la peine de mettre un tutu.**

  There's no point in putting on a tutu if you're only going to do folk dancing.

- **Le chef d'orchestre est japonais et c'est pour cela qu'il dirige avec une fourchette.**

  The conductor lost his baton when the orchestra went on strike. That's why the musicians were "Gone with the Wand" !

VOCABULARY

Coulisses = Wings	**Corpulent** = Stout
Pupitre = Music stand	**Bémol** = Flat
Baryton = Baritone	**Diva** = Diva
Blanche = Half note	**Rideau** = Curtain
Chef d'orchestre = Conductor	**Décor** = Scenery
Triple croche = Demi-semiquaver	**Loge** = Box

CHEZ LE POLITICIEN
WITH A POLITICIAN

- **Où puis-je, je vous prie, faire blanchir mon argent ?**

  Excuse me, but do you know where I can have my money laundered ?

- **Je ne veux pas vous déranger, je viens juste chercher mon vrai faux passeport.**

  I hope I'm not disturbing you. I've just come to pick up my authentic false passport.

- **Madame le Ministre, je trouve que vous avez de très beaux avantages en nature.**

  (Speaking to a female Cabinet Minister). Madam, you have some very fringe benefits.

- **Je ne pratique pas la langue de Shakespeare, mais je me débrouille assez bien avec la langue de bois.**

  I can't speak French, but I'm quite fluent in double talk.

- **J'ai une vie très saine avec de rares abus à l'exception des abus de biens sociaux.**

  I'm into clean living, except where fraudulent misuse of funds is concerned.

VOCABULARY

Découpage électoral = Warding

Retourner sa veste = To change one's colours

Prendre une veste = To come a cropper

Pot-de-vin = Bribe

Frauduleux = Fraudulent

Circonscription = Constituency

Sang contaminé = Infected blood

Corruption = Corruption

Écoute téléphonique = Wiretapping

Démagogie = Demagogy

Financement des partis = Party financing

Immunité parlementaire = Parliamentary immunity

DANS UN PHARE
IN A LIGHTHOUSE

- **Baisse un peu l'abat-jour... j'ai mal aux yeux.**

  Lower the shade a bit... my eyes hurt.

- **Les enfants, ce n'est pas de ma faute si vous ne pouvez pas jouer aux quatre coins.**

  It isn't my fault if you can't play "four corners", children.

- **Arrête de tourner en rond ! A force de te regarder, j'ai la tête qui tourne.**

  Stop going round in circles ! My head is spinning from watching you.

- **J'en ai marre ! C'est toujours moi qui raccompagne la baby-sitter...**

  I've had it ! I'm always the one who has to take the babysitter home.

- **N'oubliez pas d'éteindre en partant.**

  Don't forget to turn out the light as you leave.

VOCABULARY

Golfe = Gulf

Épave = Wreck

Bouée = Buoy

Mouette = Sea gull

Boussole = Compass

Bâbord = Port

Crique = Cove

Roulis = Rolling

Arc-en-ciel = Rainbow

Chaloupe = Launch

Tempête = Storm

Bras de mer = Inlet

CHEZ LE VÉTÉRINAIRE
AT THE VET'S

- **C'est pour mon crapaud. Il a de l'acné...**

  It's for my toad. He's got acne...

- **Pourriez-vous piquer mon abeille car je crains, hélas ! qu'elle ne soit incurable ?**

  Could you please put my bee out of its misery. It's an incurable stinger.

- **Mon caméléon est épuisé car il vient de tomber sur une couverture écossaise...**

  My chameleon is exhausted after falling on a tartan blanket.

- **Ma vache, depuis qu'elle vit en appartement, se plaint de ne plus entendre de cloches. Que dois-je faire ?**

  Since living in an apartment, my cow has been complaining about not hearing any bells ringing. What should I do ?

- **Mon héron a des varices et mon perroquet bégaie... vous pouvez faire quelque chose ?**

My heron has varicose veins and my parrot stutters. Is there anything you can do ?

VOCABULARY

Hippopotame = Hippopotamus

Congre = Conger eel

Tamanoir = Great anteater

Luciole = Firefly

Frelon = Hornet

Teckel = Dachshund

Bigorneau = Winkle

Mérou = Grouper

Chauve-souris = Bat

Limande = Dab

Canard = Duck

Cigogne = Stork

AU PARADIS
IN PARADISE

- **Excusez-moi, je suis gaucher, où se trouve la droite du Seigneur ?**

  Excuse me, but I'm left-handed. Where's the right hand of God ?

- **Où puis-je faire nettoyer mon auréole ?**

  Where can I get my halo cleaned ?

- **A quelle heure passe le prochain nuage ? J'ai une course à faire.**

  I have some errands to do. When is the next cloud scheduled to float by ?

- **J'apprécie beaucoup votre groupe de pop music, les Gregorians.**

  I really like your pop music group, the Gregorians.

- **Non merci, monsieur le serpent, je ne veux pas de pomme car je ne prends jamais de dessert.**

(Speaking to a snake) : No thank you, Sir, I don't care for an apple. I never eat dessert.

VOCABULARY

Éternel = Eternal

Céleste = Heavenly
Enfer = Hell
Zénith = Zenith
Diable = Devil
Créateur = Creator
Ange = Angel
Seigneur = Lord
Cirro-stratus = Cirrostratus
Ciel = Heaven
Divin = Divine
Galaxie = Galaxy

CHEZ LE NATIONAL SOCIALISTE
AT THE NATIONAL SOCIALIST'S

- **Dois-je garder mes bottes ou dois-je les laisser à l'entrée ?**

  May I keep my boots on or should I leave them at the door ?

- **Oh ! Votre chemise est bien plus noire que la mienne !**

  Oh, look ! Your shirt is so much blacker than mine !

- **Non merci, je ne danse pas « la danse des canards », je préfère « le pas de l'oie ».**

  No thank you, I don't do the "Bunny Hop". I prefer the "Goose Step".

- **Les petits fours étaient excellents... On voit que votre épouse ne cuisine qu'au gaz...**

  Those "petits fours" were delicious. I can see your wife only cooks with gas.

● **Laissez-moi, je vous prie, vous raccompagner jusqu'à la frontière.**

Please allow me to show you to the border.

VOCABULARY

Race = Race

Affichage sauvage = Illegal billposting

Croix gammée = Swastika

Mosquée = Mosque

Camp de concentration = Concentration camp

Mirador = Mirador

Aryen = Aryan

Treillis = Fatigues

Rangers = Combat boots

Culasse = Breech

Matraque = Truncheon

Moustache = Moustache

SUR LA LUNE
ON THE MOON

- **Faut-il changer de combinaison pour le dîner ?**

  Do I have to put on a new spacesuit for dinner ?

- **Vous avez des croissants ?**

  Do you have any crescent rolls ?

- **Où se trouve le syndicat d'initiative ?**

  Where is the tourist information bureau ?

- **A quelle heure s'envoie-t-on en l'air ?**

  When can we send each other into orbit ?

- **Cette soirée au clair de terre est vraiment romantique.**

  What a romantic evening under the earthlight !

VOCABULARY

Mésosphère = Mesosphere

Cratère = Crater

Apesanteur = Weightlessness

Éclipse = Eclipse

Lune rousse = April moon

Nébuleuse = Nebula

Astrologie = Astrology

Orbite = Orbit

Observatoire = Observatory

Navette spatiale = Space shuttle

Fusée à propergol liquide = Liquid rocket booster

Réflecteur de réservoir d'origine liquide = Lox tank baffler

AUX POMPES FUNÈBRES
AT A FUNERAL PARLOUR

- **Bonjour, je voudrais votre catalogue prin-temps-été.**

  Hello. I'd like your Spring/Summer catalogue, please.

- **Puis-je essayer vos cercueils en bois des îles ?**

  Could I try one of your coffins in exotic wood ?

- **Je souhaiterais un matelas plus dur et un oreiller plus mou.**

  I'd like a harder mattress and a softer pillow.

- **Bien que je ne sois pas très chaud pour la crémation, montrez-moi quand même vos urnes funéraires.**

  I'm not too hot on the idea of being cremated, but show me some of your funeral urns anyway.

● Je ne trouve pas que les couleurs soient très gaies ; les urnes sont-elles consignées ?

Are the urns returnable ? I don't find the colours very cheery.

VOCABULARY

Pierre tombale = Tombstone

Épitaphe = Epitaph

Trépasser = To pass away

Caveau = Vault

Cadavre = Corpse

Chrysanthème = Chrysanthemum

Corbillard = Hearse

Héritage = Inheritance

Chagrin = Sorrow

Défunt = Deceased

Couronne = Wreath

Obsèques = Funeral

Chêne = Oak

A LA BOUCHERIE
AT THE BUTCHER'S

- **Excusez-moi, madame la bouchère, mais je dois vous signaler que votre poitrine avait un drôle de goût.**

  (Speaking to the butcher's wife) : Excuse me, but I must tell you how strange your breast tasted.

- **Je crois que je vais essayer votre culotte.**

  I think I'll try your rump.

- **Je vois que vous avez deux jolis pieds de cochon. Combien coûtent-ils ?**

  I see you have two nice pig's feet. How much are they ?

- **Donnez-moi 2 kg de palette, c'est pour mon beau-frère : il est peintre.**

  I'd like 2 kilos of shoulder. I need something to cry on.

- **Bonjour, monsieur le boucher, je crois que je vais prendre vos deux oreilles et votre queue.**

  (Speaking to the butcher) : Good morning, I'd like those two ears and that tail you've got, please.

VOCABULARY

Contre-filet = Sirloin	**Biliot** = Block
Réfrigérer = To refrigerate	**Hachis** = Mince
Haut de côtes = Chuck short rib	**Saignant** = Rare
Fusil = Sharpening steel	**Jarret** = Shank
Jambonneau = Rock	**Cervelle** = Brains
Couteau à désosser = Boning knife	**Caissière** = Cashier

DANS UN AVION DE COMBAT
IN A COMBAT AIRCRAFT

- **Pourrais-je être ravitaillé en vol car je n'ai pas déjeuné ?**

  Could I be refuelled in flight since I had no lunch ?

- **Après 22 h on est prié de ne plus dépasser la vitesse du son.**

  After 10 p.m. you are asked not to go beyond the speed of sound.

- **Il y a quand même une grosse différence avec le vol à voile.**

  There is quite a big difference between this and gliding.

- **Où sont les toilettes ? Je ne me sens pas bien.**

  Where is the toilet ? I don't feel well.

- **J'ai dû confondre la poignée du signal d'alarme avec celle du siège éjectable car je ne comprends pas ce que je fais dans votre champ.**

  I can't understand what I'm doing here in your field. I must have pressed the button marked "Ejector Seat" instead of "Emergency".

VOCABULARY

Rail de lancement de missiles = Missile launch rail

Pare-brise = Windscreen

Verrière = Canopy

Volet de courbure = Flap

Caisson de voilure = Wing box

Réacteur = Jet engine

Aérofrein = Air brake

Tuyère = Exhaust nozzle

Stabilisateur = Stabiliser

Vérin de commande de volet = Flap hydraulic jack

Crosse d'appontage = Arrester hook

Perche de ravitaillement = In-flight refuelling probe

JE VAIS A LOURDES
GOING TO LOURDES

- **Je cherche le maître nageur, c'est pour la piscine.**

  I'm looking for the lifeguard. He must be at the pool.

- **A quelle heure est le prochain miracle, s'il vous plaît ?**

  When is the next miracle scheduled, please ?

- **Non merci, je ne bois que de l'eau pétillante... Je la digère mieux.**

  No thank you, I only drink bubbly water... It goes down better.

- **Je pense qu'il doit y avoir un anniversaire car je n'ai jamais vu autant de bougies.**

  It must be someone's birthday. I've never seen so many candles in all my life.

● **Vous n'auriez pas une bombe anti-crevaison ? j'ai encore crevé avec mon fauteuil roulant.**

You wouldn't happen to have a tyre repair kit, would you ? My wheelchair has got a puncture again.

VOCABULARY

Béquille commune = Underarm crutch

Béquille canadienne = Canadian crutch

Béquille d'avant-bras = Forearm crutch

Sclérose en plaques = Multiple sclerosis

Brancardier = Stretcher-bearer

Vomir = To vomit

Grotte = Grotto

Variqueux = Varicose

Procession = Procession

Canne tripode = Tripod cane

Gangrène = Gangrene

Guérison = Recovery

EN PRISON
IN PRISON

- **Où se trouve le parloir, car j'ai un rendez-vous important avec un as du barreau ?**

  Where's the visiting room please ? I have an important meeting with a top lawyer.

- **Garçon ? Ce potage est froid, soyez assez aimable pour le renvoyer aux cuisines et le faire réchauffer.**

  Waiter, this soup is cold. Would you please be so kind as to send it back to the kitchen and have it warmed up ?

- **Je ne supporte pas les rayures. Pourrais-je avoir un autre pyjama ?**

  I loathe stripes. Do you think I could have another pair of pyjamas ?

- **C'est à vous cette clef ?**

  Does this key belong to you ?

● **Je dois vous laisser car je crois que mon hélicoptère m'attend.**

I have to run. My helicopter's waiting.

VOCABULARY

Suicide = Suicide

Pendaison = Hanging

Lime = File

Injustice = Injustice

Revolver = Gun

Plaidoirie = Defence speech

Chaise électrique = Electric chair

Sursis = Suspended sentence

Évasion = Escape

Mur = Wall

Otage = Hostage

Gardien = Guard

VOCABULARY

A L'HÔTEL
AT THE HOTEL

● **la salle de bains** : the bathroom

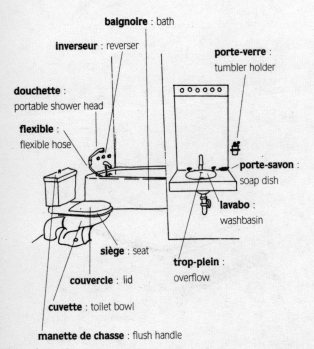

baignoire : bath

inverseur : reverser

porte-verre :
tumbler holder

douchette :
portable shower head

flexible :
flexible hose

porte-savon :
soap dish

lavabo :
washbasin

siège : seat

trop-plein :
overflow

couvercle : lid

cuvette : toilet bowl

manette de chasse : flush handle

● **cintre** : coat hanger

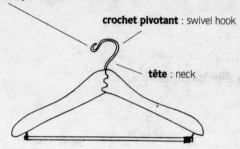

retour de protection : turnback

crochet pivotant : swivel hook

tête : neck

● **literie** : bedding

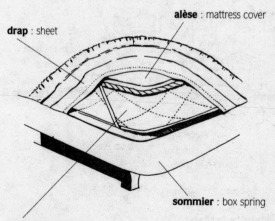

alèse : mattress cover

drap : sheet

sommier : box spring

matelas : mattress

L'INTELLECTUEL
THE INTELLECTUAL

● **chemise** : shirt

col : collar

boutonnière :
buttonhole

rabat : flap

poche poitrine :
breast pocket

manche :
sleeve

patte :
sleeve placket

gorge de chemise :
front placket

poignet : cuff

pan : shirt tail

bouton : button

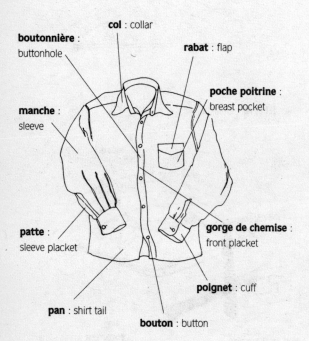

cause humanitaire :
humanitarian cause

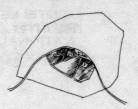

rive gauche : left bank

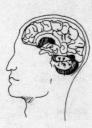

cerveau : brain

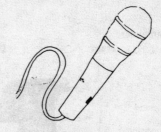

médias : media

le prix littéraire :
the literary prize

égérie : female adviser

DÉFENSE NATIONALE
NATIONAL DEFENCE

● **grenade à main :** hand grenade

ergot : lug **goupille** : safety pin

amorce : primer **anneau** : pull ring

cuiller : catch

détonateur de retard : fuse

corps en fonte : cast iron casing

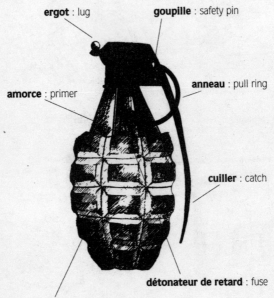

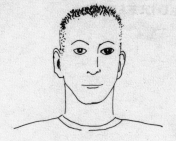

coupe de cheveux : haircut

casque : helmet

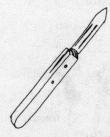

couteau à éplucher : peeler

missile sol-air :
ground to air missile

quille : demob

colombe : dove

A LA FERME
ON THE FARM

● **poule** : hen

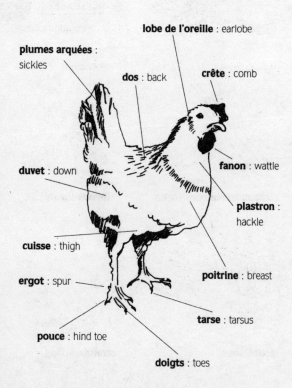

lobe de l'oreille : earlobe

plumes arquées : sickles

dos : back

crête : comb

fanon : wattle

duvet : down

plastron : hackle

cuisse : thigh

poitrine : breast

ergot : spur

tarse : tarsus

pouce : hind toe

doigts : toes

tas de fumier : manure heap

ordinateur : computer

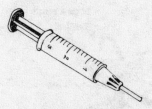

insémination : insemination

fourche : pitchfork

traite : letter of credit

traite : milking

LA RETRAITE
RETIREMENT

● **établi** : workbench

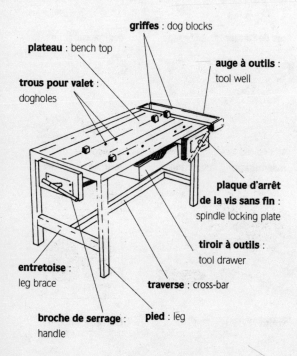

griffes : dog blocks

plateau : bench top

auge à outils : tool well

trous pour valet : dogholes

plaque d'arrêt de la vis sans fin : spindle locking plate

tiroir à outils : tool drawer

entretoise : leg brace

traverse : cross-bar

broche de serrage : handle

pied : leg

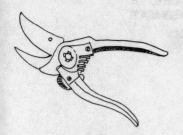

sécateur : pruning shears

télévision : television

ours en peluche : teddy bear

hameçon : hook

tricot : knitting

carte de réduction :
senior citizen's rail pass

NOËL
CHRISTMAS

● **huître** : oyster

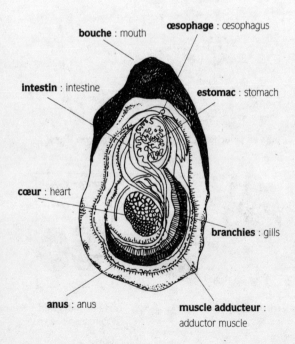

bouche : mouth

œsophage : œsophagus

intestin : intestine

estomac : stomach

cœur : heart

branchies : gills

anus : anus

muscle adducteur :
adductor muscle

cadeau : gift

cadeau : gift

bûche : log

boules : balls

l'achat des cadeaux :
buying the gifts

cadeau : gift

LA MUSIQUE
MUSIC

● **métronome** : metronome

échelle des temps : graduated scale

balancier : pendulum

curseur : weight

boîtier : box

clé de remontage : key

axe de balancier : pivot

commande marche/arrêt : on-off button

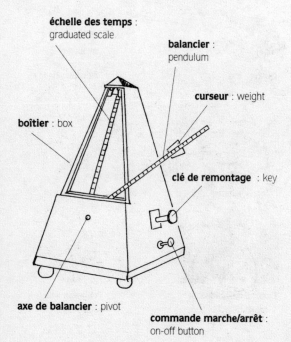

anche : reed

archet : bow

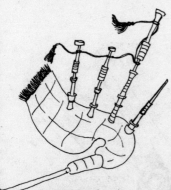

cornemuse : bagpipe

diapason : tuning fork

tambourin : tambourine

note : note

- **pince à linge** : clothes peg

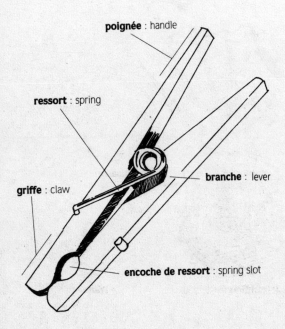

poignée : handle

ressort : spring

branche : lever

griffe : claw

encoche de ressort : spring slot

lit à baldaquin :
four-poster bed

couscoussier : couscous pot

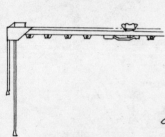

tringle à rideaux :
curtain rail

tipi : teepee

pont-levis : drawbridge

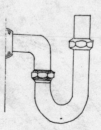

siphon : u-bend

CAMPING
TO GO CAMPING

● **couteau suisse** : Swiss army knife

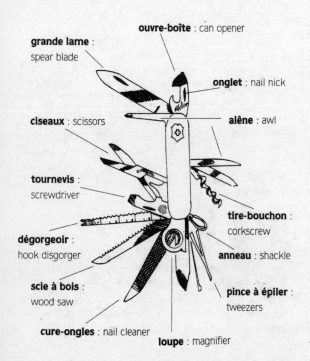

ouvre-boîte : can opener

grande lame :
spear blade

onglet : nail nick

ciseaux : scissors

alêne : awl

tournevis :
screwdriver

tire-bouchon :
corkscrew

dégorgeoir :
hook disgorger

anneau : shackle

scie à bois :
wood saw

pince à épiler :
tweezers

cure-ongles : nail cleaner

loupe : magnifier

nœud plat : reef knot

gonfleur : air pump

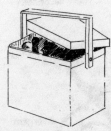

glacière : icebox

caravane : caravan

boules : bowls

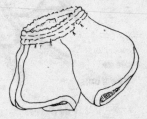

short : shorts

LA CIRCULATION
TRAFFIC

● **autoroute** : motorway

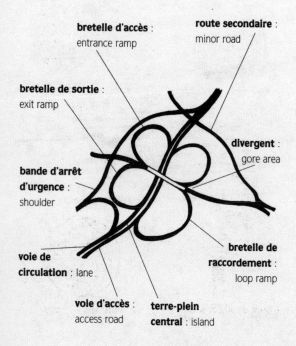

bretelle d'accès :
entrance ramp

route secondaire :
minor road

bretelle de sortie :
exit ramp

divergent :
gore area

**bande d'arrêt
d'urgence** :
shoulder

**voie de
circulation** : lane

**bretelle de
raccordement** :
loop ramp

voie d'accès :
access road

**terre-plein
central** : island

rétroviseur :
wing-mirror

aire de repos : rest area

alcootest : breathlyser

crevaison : puncture

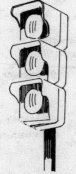

feux de signalisation :
traffic lights

vis platinées : contact points

LE LYCÉEN
HIGH SCHOOL STUDENT

● **guitare électrique** : electric guitar

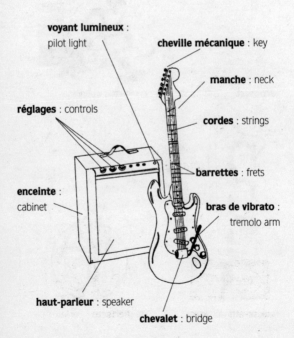

voyant lumineux :
pilot light

cheville mécanique : key

manche : neck

réglages : controls

cordes : strings

barrettes : frets

enceinte :
cabinet

bras de vibrato :
tremolo arm

haut-parleur : speaker

chevalet : bridge

moto : motorbike

tableau noir : blackboard

idole : idol

acné : acne

préservatif : condom

Perfecto : Perfecto

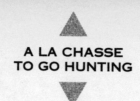

A LA CHASSE
TO GO HUNTING

● **carabine** : rifle

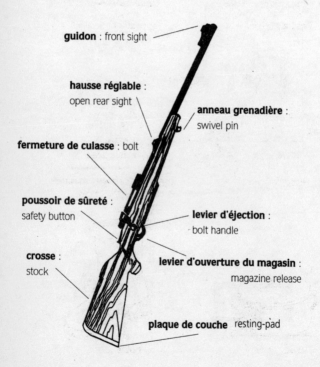

guidon : front sight

hausse réglable :
open rear sight

anneau grenadière :
swivel pin

fermeture de culasse : bolt

poussoir de sûreté :
safety button

levier d'éjection :
bolt handle

crosse :
stock

levier d'ouverture du magasin :
magazine release

plaque de couche resting-pad

collier : collar

appeau : bird call

accident : accident

passage d'animaux sauvages :
deer crossing

civet : stew

botte : boot

L'ÉNERGIE
ENERGY

- **moulin à vent** : windmill

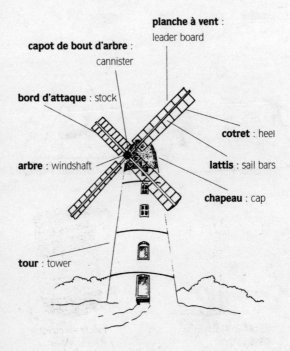

planche à vent :
leader board

capot de bout d'arbre :
cannister

bord d'attaque : stock

cotret : heel

arbre : windshaft

lattis : sail bars

chapeau : cap

tour : tower

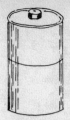

pile : battery

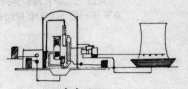

surgénérateur :
nuclear power reactor

écologiste : ecologist

soleil : sun

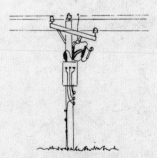

poteau électrique :
electric post

rasoir électrique :
electric shaver

AU SUPERMARCHÉ
AT THE SUPERMARKET

papier toilette : toilet paper

caisse : cash register

lait : milk

code barre : bar code

sac plastique : plastic bag

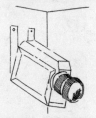

surveillance vidéo :
surveillance camera

crevettes surgelées : frozen prawns

boîte d'ananas : pineapple can

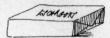

escargots surgelés : frozen snails

boîte de haricots verts : can of French beans

épinards en branches surgelés : frozen boiled spinach

boîte de tomates : canned tomatoes

CHEZ L'ANTIQUAIRE
AT THE ANTIQUE DEALER'S

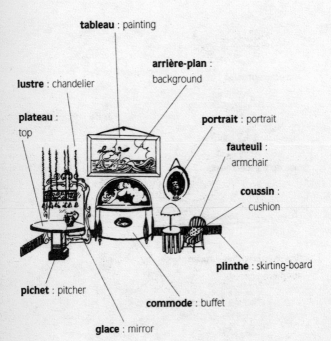

tableau : painting

arrière-plan :
background

lustre : chandelier

plateau :
top

portrait : portrait

fauteuil :
armchair

coussin :
cushion

plinthe : skirting-board

pichet : pitcher

commode : buffet

glace : mirror

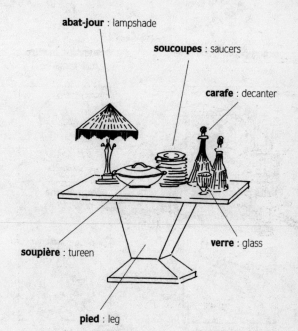

abat-jour : lampshade

soucoupes : saucers

carafe : decanter

soupière : tureen

verre : glass

pied : leg

CHÈRE FAMILLE
BELOVED FAMILY

grand-père : grandfather

fécondation in vitro :
test tube baby

belle-mère : mother-in-law

père présumé :
supposed father

pension alimentaire :
alimony

enfant du 1er lit :
child from first marriage

beau-frère : brother-in-law

gendre : son-in-law

enfant du 2e lit :
child from second marriage

belle-fille : daughter-in-law

concubin notoire :
live-in lover

arrière-grand-mère :
great-grandmother

L'ADMINISTRATION
THE ADMINISTRATION

● **bureau** : desk

plan de travail :
work surface

tiroir central :
centre drawer

retour de bureau :
return section

tirette : writing slide

caisson gauche :
left panel

pied : leg

serrure : lock

patin : floor glide

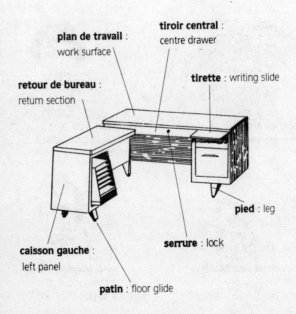

guichet : counter

magazine féminin :
women's magazine

plante verte : plant

formulaire administratif :
administrative form

mouilleur : moistener

vernis à ongles : nail polish

AU CAFÉ
AT THE CAFÉ

● **consommateur** : customer

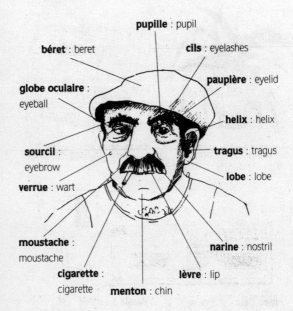

pupille : pupil

béret : beret

cils : eyelashes

globe oculaire : eyeball

paupière : eyelid

helix : helix

sourcil : eyebrow

tragus : tragus

lobe : lobe

verrue : wart

moustache : moustache

narine : nostril

cigarette : cigarette

lèvre : lip

menton : chin

œuf dur : hard-boiled egg

cartes : cards

cabinets à la turque :
turkish toilets

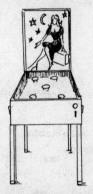

billard électrique :
pinball

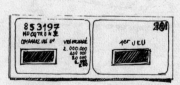

loterie : lottery

ballon de rouge :
glass of red wine

LE SPORT
SPORT

- **chaussure de course à pied** : running shoe

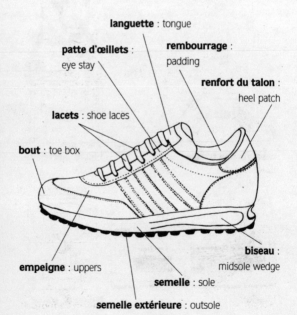

languette : tongue

patte d'œillets :
eye stay

rembourrage :
padding

renfort du talon :
heel patch

lacets : shoe laces

bout : toe box

biseau :
midsole wedge

empeigne : uppers

semelle : sole

semelle extérieure : outsole

canette de bière :
bottle of beer

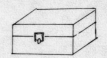

caisse noire : secret funds

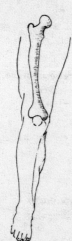

pole position : pole position

fémur : femur

volant : shuttlecock

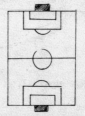

terrain de football :
soccer field

DINER EN VILLE
DINNER PARTY

● **bonne** : maid

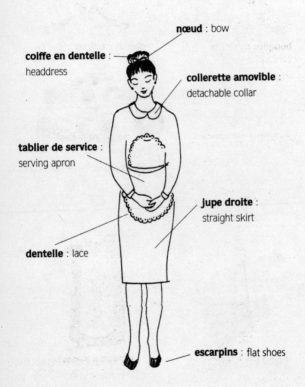

nœud : bow

coiffe en dentelle :
headdress

collerette amovible :
detachable collar

tablier de service :
serving apron

jupe droite :
straight skirt

dentelle : lace

escarpins : flat shoes

bouquet de fleurs :
bunch of flowers

nœud papillon : bow tie

rouleau à pâtisserie :
rolling pin

avocat au crabe :
avocado with crabmeat

manche à gigot :
leg of mutton handle

produit à vaisselle :
washing up liquid

WEEK-END
WEEKEND

- **toit** : roof

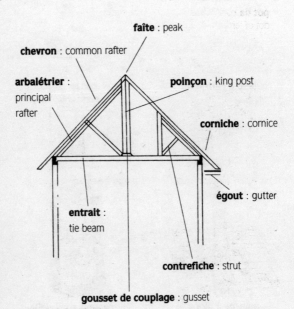

faîte : peak

chevron : common rafter

arbalétrier :
principal
rafter

poinçon : king post

corniche : cornice

égout : gutter

entrait :
tie beam

contrefiche : strut

gousset de couplage : gusset

pot de confitures :
pot of jam

chenets : fire-dogs

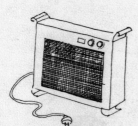

chauffage électrique :
electric heater

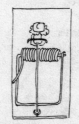

piège à souris : mousetrap

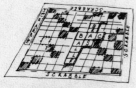

scrabble : scrabble

lampe de poche :
electric torch

LES COIFFURES
HEADGEAR

chapeau : hat

coiffe : bonnet

mitre : mitre

chapeau de mandarin :
mandarin cap

casquette : cap

chapeau de chef : chef's hat

nemès : nemès

parure de guerre : war bonnet

agal et keffieh : akal and keffiyeh

ourson : busby

calotte : yarmulke

casquette : cap

L'HOMME D'ÉTAT
STATESMAN

● **corps** : body

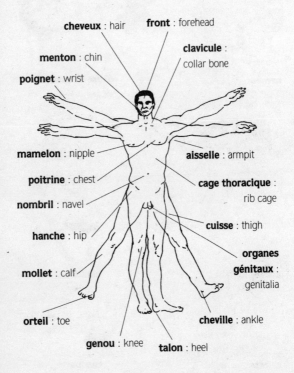

cheveux : hair   **front** : forehead

clavicule : collar bone

menton : chin

poignet : wrist

mamelon : nipple

aisselle : armpit

poitrine : chest

cage thoracique : rib cage

nombril : navel

cuisse : thigh

hanche : hip

organes génitaux : genitalia

mollet : calf

orteil : toe

cheville : ankle

genou : knee   **talon** : heel

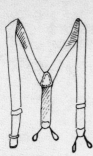

bretelles : braces

tapis rouge :
red carpet

hélicoptère : helicopter

décoration :
decoration

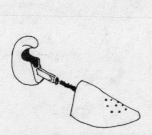

embauchoir : shoe tree

labrador : labrador

● **mouton** : sheep

carré de côtelettes : rack

garrot : withers

carré : loin

épaule :
shoulder

collet : neck

selle : rump

gigot :
leg of lamb

museau :
muzzle

tronçon :
dock

bréchet : brisket

flanc : flank

paturon : pastern

poitrine : breast

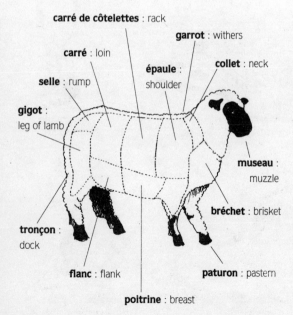

coquille Saint-Jacques : scallop **dromadaire** : dromedary

blatte : cockroach

têtard : tadpole

poisson-chat : catfish **éphémère** : mayfly

LA COMTESSE
THE COUNTESS

loden : loden

station de métro :
underground station

crocodile : crocodile

chevalière : signet ring

épingle de kilt : kilt pin

taste-vin : tasting cup

table de bridge : bridge table

robe : dress

foulard : scarf

invitations : invitations

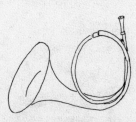

trompe de chasse : hunting horn

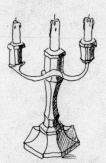

chandelier : candelabra

LA REINE
THE QUEEN

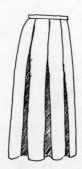

jupe : skirt

porte-jarretelles : garter belt

sac bavolet : swagger bag

face-à-main : lorgnette

agrafe : hook and eye

couvre-chaussure : overshoe

imperméable : raincoat

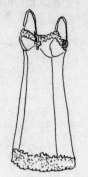

combinaison : slip

couronne : crown

capuchon : hood

collier : necklace

mouchoir : handkerchief

AU CONCOURS HIPPIQUE
AT A HORSE SHOW

- **sabots** : hooves

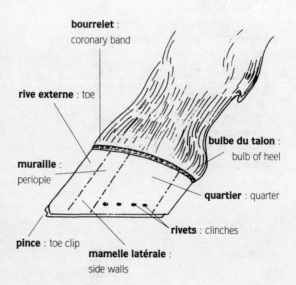

bourrelet :
coronary band

rive externe : toe

bulbe du talon :
bulb of heel

muraille :
periople

quartier : quarter

rivets : clinches

pince : toe clip

mamelle latérale :
side walls

jumelles : binoculars

capeline : wide-brimmed hat

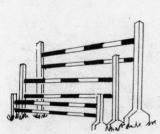

barres de spa : triple bars

étrier : stirrup

naseau : nostril

éperon : spur

LES FROMAGES
CHEESES

comté : comté

mimolette : mimolette

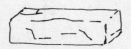

Sainte-maure : Sainte maure

bleu de Bresse :
bleu de Bresse

pont-l'évêque : pont l'évêque

saint-marcellin :
saint marcellin

camembert : camembert

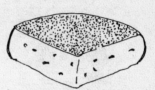

beaumont : beaumont

petit-suisse : petit suisse

valençay : valencay

gournay : gournay

emmenthal : emmenthal

AUX SPORTS D'HIVER
WINTER SPORTS RESORT

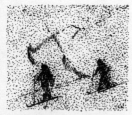

brouillard : fog

neige : snow

école de ski : ski school

fanion : flag

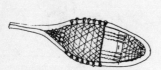

raquette : snowshoe

moufle : mitt

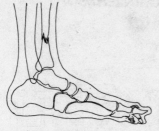

fracture : fracture

grog : grog

remonte-pente : skilift

pylône : pylon

la montée : climbing

la montée : climbing

L'HOMME D'AFFAIRES
THE BUSINESSMAN

portrait de famille :
family portrait

carte de crédit : credit card

sole meunière :
sole meuniere

secrétaire : secretary

trombone : paper clip

voiture : car

billet d'avion : plane ticket

lunettes : glasses

bible : bible

tee de golf : golf tee

chemise rayée : striped shirt

maîtresse : mistress

GLOSSAIRE FRANÇAIS-ANGLAIS
FRENCH-ENGLISH GLOSSARY

- **Abaisse-langue** :
  Tongue depressor
- **Abat-jour** : Lampshade
- **Abside** : Apse
- **Accident** : Accident
- **Achat des cadeaux (l')** :
  Buying the gifts
- **Acné** : Acne
- **Action** : Share
- **Aérofrein** : Air brake
- **Affichage sauvage** :
  Illegal billposting
- **Agal** : Akal
- **Agrafe** : Hook and eye
- **Aiguillage** : Switch
- **Aire de repos** : Rest area
- **Aisselle** : Armpit
- **Alcootest** : Breathlyser
- **Alêne** : Awl
- **Alèse** : Mattress cover
- **Alphabet** : Alphabet
- **Amorce** : Primer
- **Anche** : Reed
- **Anémomachmètre** :
  Mach and speed indicator
- **Ange** : Angel
- **Anneau** : Pull ring
- **Anneau** : Shackle
- **Anneau grenadière** :
  Swivel pin
- **Anus** : Anus
- **Apesanteur** :
  Weightlessness
- **Appeau** : Bird call
- **Arbalétrier** : Principal rafter
- **Arbre** : Windshaft

- **Arbre turbine compresseur** :
  Turbine compressor shaft
- **Arc-boutant** : Flying Buttress
- **Archet** : Bow
- **Arc-en-ciel** : Rainbow
- **Arrière-grand-mère** :
  Great-grandmother
- **Arrière-plan** : Background
- **Aryen** : Aryan
- **Astrologie** : Astrology
- **Aube** : Alb
- **Auge à outils** : Tool well
- **Autoroute** : Motorway
- **Avocat** : Lawyer
- **Avocat au crabe** :
  Avocado with crabmeat
- **Axe de balancier** : Pivot

- **Bâbord** : Port
- **Baignoire** : Bath
- **Balancier** : Pendulum
- **Ballon de rouge** :
  Glass of red wine
- **Bande d'arrêt d'urgence** :
  Hard shoulder
- **Barre de maintien** :
  Side handrail
- **Barre de plongée** :
  Starboard diving plane
- **Barres de spa** : Triple bars
- **Barrettes** : Frets
- **Baryton** : Baritone
- **Bavure** : Unfortunate mistake
- **Beau-frère** : Brother-in-law
- **Beaumont** : Beaumont

- **Belle-fille** : Daughter-in-law
- **Belle-mère** : Mother-in-law
- **Bémol** : Flat
- **Bénitier** : Stoup
- **Béquille canadienne** :
  Canadian crutc
- **Béquille commune** :
  Underarm crutch
- **Béquille d'avant-bras** :
  Forearm crutch
- **Béret** : Beret
- **Bible** : Bible
- **Bigorneau** : Winkle
- **Bigot** : Holier-than-thou
- **Billard électrique** : Pinball
- **Billet d'avion** : Plane ticket
- **Billot** : Block
- **Biseau** : Midsole wedge
- **Blanche** : Half note
- **Blatte** : Cockroach
- **Bleu de Bresse** :
  Bleu de Bresse
- **Boîte d'ananas** :
  Pineapple can
- **Boîte de haricots verts** :
  Can of French beans
- **Boîte de tomates** :
  Canned tomatoes
- **Boîtier** : Box
- **Bol** : Bowl
- **Bombe atomique** :
  Nuclear bomb
- **Bonne** : Maid
- **Bord d'attaque** : Stock
- **Borderline** : Borderline
- **Botte** : Boot
- **Bouche** : Mouth
- **Bouée** : Buoy
- **Boules** : Bowls
- **Bouquet de fleurs** :
  Bunch of flowers
- **Bourrelet** : Coronary band
- **Bourse** : Stock Exchange
- **Boussole** : Compass
- **Bout** : Toe box
- **Boutique hors taxe** :
  Duty free shop
- **Bouton** : Button
- **Boutonnière** : Buttonhole
- **Brancardier** : Stretcher-bearer

- **Branche** : Levier
- **Branchies** : Gills
- **Bras de mer** : Inlet
- **Bras de vibrato** :
  Tremolo arm
- **Bréchet** : Brisket
- **Bretelle d'accès** :
  Entrance ramp
- **Bretelle de raccordement** :
  Loop ramp
- **Bretelle de sortie** :
  Exit ramp
- **Bretelles** : Braces
- **Broche de serrage** : Handle
- **Bronzer** : To get a tan
- **Brouillard** : Fog
- **Bûche** : Log
- **Bulbe du talon** : Bulb of heel
- **Bureau** : Desk
- **Butoir** : Bumper

- **Cabinets à la turque** :
  Turkish toilets
- **Cachalot** : Sperm whale
- **Cachet** : Tablet
- **Cadavre** : Corpse
- **Cadeau** : Gift
- **Cage thoracique** : Rib cage
- **Caisse** : Car
- **Caisse** : Cash register
- **Caisse noire** : Secret funds
- **Caissier** : Cashier
- **Caissière** : Cashier
- **Caisson de voilure** :
  Wing box
- **Caisson gauche** :
  Left panel
- **Calotte** : Yarmulke
- **Camembert** : Camembert
- **Camp de concentration** :
  Concentration camp
- **Canard** : Duck
- **Canard laqué** : Peking duck
- **Canette de bière** :
  Bottle of beer
- **Canne tripode** : Tripod cane
- **Capeline** : Wide-brimmed hat
- **Capot de bout d'arbre** :
  Cannister

- **Capuchon** : Hood
- **Carabine** : Rifle
- **Carafe** : Decanter
- **Caravane** : Caravan
- **Carpe** : Carpus
- **Carré** : Loin
- **Carré de côtelettes** : Rack
- **Carte de crédit** : Credit card
- **Carte de réduction** :
  Senior citizen's rail pass
- **Cartes** : Cards
- **Casque** : Helmet
- **Casquette** : Cap
- **Catastrophe aérienne** :
  Plane crash
- **Cause humanitaire** :
  Humanitarian cause
- **Caveau** : Vault
- **Ceinturon** : Belt
- **Céleste** : Heavenly
- **Cerf-volant** : Kite
- **Cerveau** : Brain
- **Chagrin** : Sorrow
- **Chaise électrique** :
  Electric chair
- **Chaloupe** : Launch
- **Chambre des machines** :
  Engine room
- **Chandelier** : Candelabra
- **Chape** : Cope
- **Chapeau** : Hat
- **Chapeau** : Cap
- **Chapeau de mandarin** :
  Mandarin cap
- **Chapitre** : Chapter
- **Chariot à bagage** :
  Baggage cart
- **Chasteté** : Chastity
- **Chasuble** : Chasuble
- **Chat-huant** : Screech owl
- **Chaudière** : Boiler
- **Chauffage électrique** :
  Electric heater
- **Chaussure de course à pied** :
  Running shoe
- **Chauve-souris** . Bat
- **Chef d'orchestre** : Conductor
- **Chemise** : Shirt
- **Chemise rayée** : Striped shirt
- **Chenets** : Andirons

- **Chêne** : Oak
- **Chèque** : Cheque
- **Chevalet** : Bridge
- **Chevalière** : Signet ring
- **Cheveux** : Hair
- **Cheville** : Ankle
- **Cheville mécanique** : Key
- **Chevron** : Common rafter
- **Chinchilla** : Chinchilla
- **Chrysanthème** :
  Chrysanthemum
- **Ciel** : Heaven
- **Cigarette** : Cigarette
- **Cigogne** : Stork
- **Cils** : Eyelashes
- **Cintre** : Coat hanger
- **Circonscription** :
  Constituency
- **Cirro-stratus** : Cirrostratus
- **Ciseaux** : Scissors
- **Civet** : Stew
- **Clavicule** : Collar bone
- **Clef de voûte** : Keystone
- **Cloche** : Bell
- **Clocher** : Bell tower
- **Cloître** : Cloister
- **Code barre** : Bar code
- **Cœur** : Heart
- **Coffre-fort** : Safe
- **Coiffe** : Bonnet
- **Coiffe en dentelle** :
  Headdress
- **Col** : Collar
- **Collerette amovible** :
  Detachable collar
- **Collet** : Neck
- **Collier** : Collar
- **Collier** : Necklace
- **Colombe** : Dove
- **Combinaison** : Slip
- **Commande marche/arrêt** :
  On-off button
- **Commode** : Buffet
- **Complément** : Complement
- **Comté** : Comté
- **Concile** : Synod
- **Conclave** : Conclave
- **Concubin notoire** :
  Live-in lover
- **Congre** : Conger eel

- **Consommateur** : Customer
- **Consonne** : Consonant
- **Contravention** : Fine
- **Contrefiche** : Strut
- **Contre-filet** : Sirloin
- **Coquille Saint-Jacques** :
  Scallop
- **Corbillard** : Hearse
- **Cordes** : Strings
- **Cornemuse** : Bagpipe
- **Corniche** : Cornice
- **Corps** : Body
- **Corps en fonte** :
  Cast iron casing
- **Corpulent** : Stout
- **Corruption** : Corruption
- **Cotret** : Heel
- **Couchette** : Bunk
- **Coulisses** : Wings
- **Coupe de cheveux** : Haircut
- **Courbette** : Low bow
- **Couronne** : Crown
- **Couronne** : Wreath
- **Couscoussier** : Couscous pot
- **Coussin** : Cushion
- **Couteau à désosser** :
  Boning knife
- **Couteau à éplucher** : Peeler
- **Couteau suisse** : Swiss army knife
- **Couvent** : Convent
- **Couvercle** : Cover
- **Couverture écossaise** :
  Tartan blanket
- **Couvre-chaussure** : Overshoe
- **Crâne** : Skull
- **Cratère** : Crater
- **Créancier** : Creditor
- **Créateur** : Creator
- **Crédit** : Credit
- **Crête** : Crest
- **Crête** : Comb
- **Crevaison** : Puncture
- **Crevette** : Prawn
- **Crevettes surgelées** :
  Frozen prawns
- **Crique** : Cove
- **Crochet pivotant** :
  Swivel hook
- **Crocodile** : Crocodile
- **Croix gammée** : Swastika

- **Crosse** : Crosier
- **Crosse** : Stock
- **Crosse d'appontage** :
  Arrester hook
- **Cubitus** : Ulna
- **Cuiller** : Catch
- **Cuisse** : Thigh
- **Culasse** : Breech
- **Cumulo-nimbus** :
  Cumulonimbus
- **Cure-dent** : Toothpick
- **Cure-ongles** : Nail cleaner
- **Curseur** : Key
- **Cuvette** : Toilet bowl

- **Débiteur** : Debtor
- **Décalage horaire** : Jet lag
- **Décollage** : Takeoff
- **Décor** : Scenery
- **Décoration** : Decoration
- **Découpage électoral** :
  Warding
- **Défunt** : Deceased
- **Dégorgeoir** : Hook disgorger
- **Démagogie** : Demagogy
- **Dentelle** : Lace
- **Détonateur de retard** :
  Fuse
- **Détournement** : Hijacking
- **Dévotion** : Devotion
- **Diable** : Devil
- **Diapason** : Tuning fork
- **Diocèse** : Diocese
- **Diva** : Diva
- **Divergent** : Gore area
- **Divin** : Divine
- **Doigts** : Toes
- **Dos** : Back
- **Douchette** :
  Portable shower head
- **Drap** : Sheet
- **Dromadaire** : Dromedary
- **Dune** : Dune
- **Duvet** : Down

- **Échelle des temps** :
  Graduated scale
- **Éclipse** : Eclipse

- **École de ski** : Ski school
- **Écologiste** : Ecologist
- **Écoute téléphonique** : Wiretapping
- **Écume** : Foam
- **Écumoire** : Skimmer
- **Égérie** : Egeria
- **Égout** : Sewer
- **Embauchoir** : Shoe tree
- **Embruns** : Sea spray
- **Emmenthal** : Emmenthal
- **Empeigne** : Uppers
- **Empereur** : Emperor
- **Enceinte** : Cabinet
- **Encoche de ressort** : Spring slot
- **Encyclique** : Encyclical
- **Enfant du 1er lit** : Child from first marriage
- **Enfant du 2e lit** : Child from second marriage
- **Enfer** : Hell
- **Enflure** : Creep
- **Entrait** : Tie beam
- **Entretoise** : Leg brace
- **Épargne** : Savings
- **Épaule** : Shoulder
- **Épave** : Wreck
- **Épeler** : To spell
- **Éperon** : Spur
- **Éphémère** : Mayfly
- **Épinards en branches surgelés** : Frozen boiled spinach
- **Épingle de kilt** : Kilt pin
- **Épitaphe** : Epitaph
- **Épithète** : Epithet
- **Ergot** : Lug
- **Ergot** : Spur
- **Erreur humaine** : Creep
- **Escalier mécanique** : Escalator
- **Escargots surgelés** : Frozen snails
- **Escarpins** : Pumps
- **Escompte** : Discount
- **Estomac** : Stomach
- **Esturgeon** : Sturgeon
- **Établi** : Workbench
- **Éternel** : Eternal

- **Étole** : Stole
- **Étrier** : Stirrup
- **Évasion** : Escape
- **Extase** : Ecstasy

- **Face-à-main** : Lorgnette
- **Faillite** : Bankruptcy
- **Faîte** : Peak
- **Fanion** : Flag
- **Fanon** : Wattle
- **Fantasme** : Fantasy
- **Fauteuil** : Armchair
- **Fauteuil roulant** : Wheelchair
- **Fécondation in vitro** : Test tube baby
- **Fémur** : Femur
- **Fermeture de culasse** : Bolt
- **Feux de signalisation** : Traffic lights
- **Financement des partis** : Party financing
- **Flanc** : Flank
- **Flèche** : Spire
- **Flexible** : Flexible hose
- **Foi** : Faith
- **Formulaire administratif** : Administrative form
- **Foulard** : Scarf
- **Fourche** : Pitchfork
- **Fracture** : Fracture
- **Frauduleux** : Fraudulent
- **Frelon** : Hornet
- **Front** : Forehead
- **Fusée à propergol liquide** : Liquid rocket booster
- **Fusil** : Sharpening steel

- **Galaxie** : Galaxy
- **Galère** : Bore
- **Galet** : Pebble
- **Gangrène** : Gangrene
- **Gardien** : Guard
- **Garrot** : Withers
- **Gendre** : Son-in-law
- **Genou** : Knee
- **Gigot** : Leg of lamb
- **Gingembre** : Ginger

- **Glace** : Mirror
- **Glacière** : Icebox
- **Globe oculaire** : Eyeball
- **Glossaire** : Glossary
- **Goémon** : Wrack
- **Golfe** : Gulf
- **Gonfleur** : Air pump
- **Gorge de chemise** :
  Front placket
- **Goupille** : Safety pin
- **Gournay** : Gournay
- **Gousset de couplage** :
  Gusset
- **Gouvernail de plongée avant** :
  Port sail plane
- **Grand-père** : Grandfather
- **Grande lame** : Spear blade
- **Grenade à main** :
  Hand grenade
- **Griffe** : Claw
- **Griffes** : Dog blocks
- **Grog** : Grog
- **Grotte** : Grotto
- **Guérison** : Recovery
- **Guichet** : Counter
- **Guidon** : Front sight
- **Guitare électrique** :
  Electric guitar

- **Hachis** : Mince
- **Hameçon** : Hook
- **Hanche** : Hip
- **Hareng** : Herring
- **Hausse réglable** :
  Open rear sight
- **Haut de côtes** :
  Chuck short rib
- **Haut-parleur** : Speaker
- **Hélice** : Propeller
- **Hélicoptère** : Helicopter
- **Helix** : Helix
- **Héritage** : Inheritance
- **Hippopotame** :
  Hippopotamus
- **Honda** : Honda
- **Honte (la)** : Shame
- **Huître** : Oyster

- **Idole** : Idol
- **Ilion** : Ilium
- **Immigré** : Immigrant
- **Immunité parlementaire** :
  Parliamentary immunity
- **Imperméable** : Raincoat
- **Infaillibilité** : Infallibility
- **Infirmière** : Nurse
- **Injustice** : Injustice
- **Innocent** : Innocent
- **Insémination** : Insemination
- **Instruments de vol** :
  Flying instruments
- **Intestin** : Intestine
- **Inverseur** : Reverser
- **Invitations** : Invitations

- **Jarret** : Shank
- **Jaune** : Yellow
- **Jumelles** : Binoculars
- **Jupe** : Skirt
- **Jupe droite** : Straight skirt

- **Keffieh** : Keffyeh
- **Kiosque** : Conning tower

- **Labrador** : Labrador
- **Lacets** : Shoe laces
- **Lait** : Milk
- **Lampe de poche** :
  Electric torch
- **Lamproie** : Lamprey
- **Languette** : Tongue
- **Lattis** : Sail bars
- **Lavabo** : Washbasin
- **Levier d'éjection** : Bolt
  handle
- **Levier d'ouverture du
  magasin** :
  Magazine release
- **Lèvre** : Lip
- **Lézard** : Problem
- **Limande** : Dab
- **Lime** : File
- **Literie** : Bedding
- **Lit à baldaquin** :
  Four-poster bed

- **Lobe** : Lobe
- **Lobe de l'oreille** : Earlobe
- **Loden** : Loden
- **Loge** : Box
- **Loterie** : Lottery
- **Loupe** : Magnifier
- **Luciole** : Firefly
- **Lune rousse** : April moon
- **Lunettes** : Glasses
- **Lustre** : Chandelier
- **Luxe** : Luxury

- **Machine à écrire** : Typewriter
- **Magazine féminin** :
  Women's magazine
- **Magot** : Pile
- **Maître d'hôtel** : Butler
- **Maîtresse** : Mistress
- **Malléole** : Calcaneus
- **Mamelle latérale** : Side walls
- **Mamelon** : Nipple
- **Manche** : Neck
- **Manche** : Sleeve
- **Manche à gigot** :
  Leg of mutton handle
- **Manette de chasse** :
  Flush handle
- **Mangouste** : Mongoose
- **Matelas** : Mattress
- **Matraque** : Truncheon
- **Médias** : Media
- **Méditation** : Meditation
- **Méduse** : Jellyfish
- **Menton** : Chin
- **Menu** : Menu
- **Mérou** : Grouper
- **Mésosphère** : Mesosphere
- **Metatarse** : Metatarsal
- **Métronome** : Metronome
- **Mimolette** : Mimolette
- **Mirador** : Mirador
- **Missile** : Missile
- **Missile sol-air** :
  Ground to air missile
- **Mitre** : Miter
- **Moine** : Monk
- **Mollet** : Calf
- **Montée** : Climbing
- **Mosquée** : Mosque

- **Mot** : Word
- **Moto** : Motorbike
- **Motrice** : Motor unit lever
- **Mouchoir** : Handkerchief
- **Mouette** : Sea gull
- **Moufle** : Mitt
- **Mouilleur** : Moistener
- **Moulin à vent** : Windmill
- **Moustache** : Moustache
- **Mouton** : Sheep
- **Mule** : Mule
- **Mur** : Wall
- **Muraille** : Periople
- **Muscle adducteur** :
  Adductor muscle
- **Museau** : Muzzle

- **Narcissique** : Narcissistic
- **Narine** : Nostril
- **Naseau** : Nostril
- **Navette spatiale** :
  Space shuttle
- **Nébuleuse** : Nebula
- **Nef** : Nave
- **Neige** : Snow
- **Nemès** : Nemès
- **Névrotique** : Neurotic
- **Nœud** : Bow
- **Nœud papillon** : Bow tie
- **Nœud plat** : Reef knot
- **Nombril** : Navel
- **Nonce** : Nuncio
- **Note** : Note
- **Novice** : Novice

- **Obligation** : Bond
- **Obsèques** : Funeral
- **Observatoire** : Observatory
- **Œdipe** : Œdipus
- **Œsophage** : Œsophagus
- **Œuf dur** : Hard-boiled egg
- **Omoplate** : Shoulder blade
- **Onglet** : Nail nick
- **Ordinateur** : Computer
- **Or** : Gold
- **Orbite** : Orbit
- **Organes génitaux** : Genitalia
- **Orignal** : Moose

- **Orteil** : Toe
- **Otage** : Hostage
- **Oto-rhino-laryngologiste** :
  Ear, nose and throat specialist
- **Ourson** : Busby
- **Ours en peluche** : Teddy bear
- **Ouvre-boîte** : Can opener
- **Ovaire** : Ovary

- **Pan de chemise** : Shirt tail
- **Papier toilette** : Toilet paper
- **Parasol** : Beach umbrella
- **Pare-brise** : Windshield
- **Parloir** : Parlour
- **Parure de guerre** :
  War bonnet
- **Passage d'animaux
  sauvages** : Deer crossing
- **Patibulaire** : Sinister
- **Patin** : Floor glide
- **Patte** : Sleeve placket
- **Patte d'œillets** : Eye stay
- **Paturon** : Pastern
- **Paupière** : Eyelid
- **Pendaison** : Hanging
- **Pénis** : Penis
- **Pension alimentaire** :
  Alimony
- **Perche de ravitaillement** :
  In-flight refuelling probe
- **Père présumé** :
  Supposed father
- **Perfecto** : Perfecto
- **Péroné** : Fibula
- **Pétard** : Joint
- **Petit-suisse** : Petit suisse
- **Phallique** : Phallic
- **Phobique** : Phobic
- **Pichet** : Pitcher
- **Pied** : Leg
- **Piège à souris** : Mousetrap
- **Pierre tombale** :
  Tombstone
- **Pile** : Battery
- **Pince** : Toe clip
- **Pince à épiler** : Tweezers
- **Pince à linge** : Clothes pin
- **Plaidoirie** : Defence speech
- **Planche à vent** : Leader board

- **Plan de travail** : Work surface
- **Plante verte** : Plant
- **Plaque d'arrêt de la vis
  sans fin** : Spindle locking plate
- **Plaque de couche antérieure** :
  Record pad
- **Plaqué or** : Gold plate
- **Plastron** : Hackle
- **Plateau** : Bench top
- **Plateau** : Top
- **Pléonasme** : Pleonasm
- **Plinthe** : Plinth
- **Plumes arquées** : Sickles
- **Pluriel** : Plural
- **Poche poitrine** :
  Breast pocket
- **Poignée** : Handle
- **Poignet** : Cuff
- **Poignet** : Wrist
- **Poinçon** : King post
- **Poisson-chat** : Catfish
- **Poisson cru** : Raw fish
- **Poitrine** : Breast
- **Poitrine** : Chest
- **Pole position** : Pole position
- **Pont-l'évêque** : Pont l'évêque
- **Pont-levis** : Drawbridge
- **Porte-jarretelles** : Garter belt
- **Porte-savon** : Soap dish
- **Porte-verre** : Tumbler holder
- **Portes coulissantes** :
  Sliding doors
- **Portrait** : Portrait
- **Portrait de famille** :
  Family portrait
- **Pot de confitures** :
  Pot of jam
- **Pot-de-vin** : Bribe
- **Poteau électrique** :
  Electric post
- **Pou** : Louse
- **Pouce** : Hind toe
- **Poule** : Hen
- **Poussoir de sûreté** :
  Safety button
- **Pouvoir** : Power
- **Prendre une veste** :
  To come a cropper
- **Préservatif** : Condom
- **Prise de tête** : Real pain

- **Prix littéraire** : Literary prize
- **Procession** : Procession
- **Produit à vaisselle** :
  Washing up liquid
- **Projection** : Projection
- **Prostate** : Prostate
- **Pulsion** : Drive
- **Pupille** : Pupil
- **Pupitre** : Music stand
- **Putois** : Polecat
- **Pylône** : Pylon

- **Quai** : Platform
- **Quartier** : Quarter
- **Quille** : Demob

- **Rabat** : Flap
- **Race** : Race
- **Radiographie** : X-ray
- **Rail de lancement de
  missiles** : Missile launch rail
- **Rame** : Train
- **Rangers** : Combat boots
- **Raquette** : Snowshoe
- **Rasoir électrique** :
  Electric shaver
- **Réacteur** : Jet engine
- **Réacteur** : Reactor
- **Réflecteur de réservoir
  d'origine liquide** :
  Lox tank baffler
- **Réfrigérer** : To refrigerate
- **Réglages** : Controls
- **Régression** : Regression
- **Rembourrage** : Padding
- **Remonte-pente** : Skilift
- **Renfort du talon** : Heel patch
- **Ressort** : Spring
- **Retour de bureau** :
  Return section
- **Retour de protection** :
  Turnback
- **Retourner sa veste** :
  To turn one's coat
- **Rétroviseur** :
  Rear view mirror
- **Revolver** : Gun
- **Rideau** : Curtain

- **Rive externe** : Toe
- **Rive gauche** : Left bank
- **Rivets** : Clinches
- **Riz cantonais** : Fried rice
- **Rizière** : Ricefield
- **Robe** : Dress
- **Rotule** : Knee cap
- **Rouleau à pâtisserie** :
  Rolling pin
- **Rouleau de printemps** :
  Spring roll
- **Roulis** : Rolling
- **Route secondaire** :
  Minor road

- **Sabots** : Hooves
- **Sacrum** : Sacrum
- **Sac bavolet** : Swagger bag
- **Sac plastique** : Plastic bag
- **Saignant** : Rare
- **Saint-marcellin** :
  Saint marcellin
- **Sainte-maure** : Sainte maure
- **Salle de bains** : Bathroom
- **Sang contaminé** :
  Infected blood
- **Sangsue** : Leech
- **Sapé** : Dressed
- **Sas d'accès arrière** :
  Air lock
- **Schizophrénie** :
  Schizophrenia
- **Scie à bois** : Wood saw
- **Sclérose en plaques** :
  Multiple sclerosis
- **Scrabble** : Scrabble
- **Sécateur** : Pruning shears
- **Secrétaire** : Secretary
- **Seigneur** : Lord
- **Selle** : Rump
- **Semelle** : Sole
- **Semelle extérieure** : Outsole
- **Seringue** : Syringe
- **Serrure** : Lock
- **Short** : Shorts
- **Siège** : Seat
- **Signal d'alarme** :
  Emergency brake
- **Silure** : Silurid

- **Singulier** : Singular
- **Siphon** : U-bend
- **Sole meunière** :
  Sole meuniere
- **Soleil** : Sun
- **Sommier** : Box spring
- **Soucoupes** : Saucers
- **Soupe** : Soup
- **Soupière** : Tureen
- **Sourcil** : Eyebrow
- **Soutien-gorge** : Bra
- **Spéculation** : Speculation
- **Spéculer** : To speculate
- **Spéculum** : Speculum
- **Stabilisateur** : Stabilizer
- **Station de métro** :
  Underground station
- **Sternum** : Sternum
- **Stimulateur cardiaque** :
  Pacemaker
- **Suicide** : Suicide
- **Surgénérateur** :
  Nuclear power reactor
- **Surplis** : Surplice
- **Sursis** :
  Suspended sentence
- **Surveillance vidéo** :
  Video supervision
- **Survivant** : Survivor

- **Table de bridge** :
  Bridge table
- **Tableau** : Painting
- **Tableau noir** : Blackboard
- **Tablier de service** :
  Serving apron
- **Talon** : Heel
- **Tamanoir** : Great anteater
- **Tambourin** : Tambourine
- **Tapir** : Tapir
- **Tapis rouge** : Red carpet
- **Tarse** : Tarsus
- **Tas de fumier** : Manure heap
- **Taste-vin** : Tasting cup
- **Teckel** : Dachshund
- **Tee de golf** : Golf tee
- **Télévision** : Television
- **Tempête** : Storm
- **Temple** : Temple

- **Terrain de football** :
  Soccer field
- **Terre-plein central** : Island
- **Fêtard** : Tadpole
- **Tête** : Neck
- **Thé** : Tea
- **Tipi** : Teepee
- **Tire-bouchon** : Corkscrew
- **Tirette** : Writing slide
- **Tiroir à outils** : Tool drawer
- **Tiroir central** :
  Centre drawer
- **Toit** : Roof
- **Toque de chef** : Chef's hat
- **Torpille** : Torpedo
- **Tour** : Tower
- **Tournevis** : Screwdriver
- **Tourniquet** : Turnstile
- **Tragus** : Tragus
- **Traite** : Letter of credit
- **Traite** : Milking
- **Traverse** : Crossbar
- **Traverse** : Sleeper
- **Treillis** : Fatigue dress
- **Tremblement de terre** :
  Earthquake
- **Trépasser** : To pass away
- **Tricot** : Knitting
- **Tringle à rideaux** :
  Curtain rail
- **Triple croche** :
  Demi-semiquaver
- **Trombone** : Paper clip
- **Trompe de chasse** :
  Hunting horn
- **Tronc** : Collection box
- **Tronche de cake** : Jerk
- **Tronçon** : Dock
- **Trop** : Too much
- **Trop-plein** : Overflow
- **Trou d'air** : Air pocket
- **Trous pour valet** : Dogholes
- **Truffe** : Truffle
- **Tube lance-missiles** :
  Missile tube
- **Tuyère** : Exhaust nozzle

- **Valençay** : Valencay
- **Vapeur** : Steam
- **Variqueux** : Varicose

- **Veine cave supérieure** :
  Superior vena cava
- **Vent arrière** : Rear wind
- **Verbe** : Verb
- **Vérin de commande de volet** :
  Flap hydraulic jack
- **Vernis à ongles** : Nail polish
- **Verre** : Glass
- **Verrière** : Canopy
- **Verrue** : Wart
- **Vessie** : Bladder
- **Vicaire** : Curate
- **Viol** : Rape
- **Violon** : Prison
- **Visière** : Peak
- **Vison** : Mink
- **Vis platinées** : Contact points
- **Vœu** : Vow
- **Voie** : Track
- **Voie d'accès** : Access road
- **Voie de circulation** : Lane
- **Voiture** : Car
- **Volant** : Shuttlecock
- **Volet de courbure** : Flap
- **Vomir** : To vomit
- **Voussure** : Arch
- **Voyant lumineux** : Pilot light
- **Voyelle** : Vowel

- **Wok** : Wok

- **Yacht** : Yacht
- **Yamaha** : Yamaha
- **Yeux bridés** : Slanting eyes

- **Zénith** : Zenith
- **Zoner** : To wander around

GLOSSAIRE ANGLAIS-FRANÇAIS
ENGLISH-FRENCH GLOSSARY

- **Access road** : Voie d'accès
- **Accident** : Accident
- **Acne** : Acné
- **Adductor muscle** :
  Muscle adducteur
- **Administrative form** :
  Formulaire administratif
- **Air brake** : Aérofrein
- **Air lock** : Sas d'accès arrière
- **Air pocket** : Trou d'air
- **Air pump** : Gonfleur
- **Akal** : Agal
- **Alb** : Aube
- **Alimony** :
  Pension alimentaire
- **Alphabet** : Alphabet
- **Angel** : Ange
- **Ankle** : Cheville
- **Anus** : Anus
- **April moon** : Lune rousse
- **Apse** : Abside
- **Arch** : Voussure
- **Armchair** : Fauteuil
- **Armpit** : Aisselle
- **Arrester hook** :
  Crosse d'appontage
- **Aryan** : Aryen
- **Astrology** : Astrologie
- **Avocado with crabmeat** :
  Avocat au crabe
- **Awl** : Alêne

- **Back** : Dos
- **Background** : Arrière-plan
- **Baggage cart** :
  Chariot à bagage
- **Bagpipe** : Cornemuse

- **Bankruptcy** : Faillite
- **Bar code** : Code barre
- **Baritone** : Baryton
- **Bat** : Chauve-souris
- **Bathroom** : Salle de bains
- **Bath** : Baignoire
- **Battery** : Pile
- **Beach umbrella** : Parasol
- **Beaumont** : Beaumont
- **Bedding** : Literie
- **Bell** : Cloche
- **Bell tower** : Clocher
- **Belt** : Ceinturon
- **Bench top** : Plateau
- **Beret** : Béret
- **Bible** : Bible
- **Binoculars** : Jumelles
- **Bird call** : Appeau
- **Blackboard** : Tableau noir
- **Bladder** : Vessie
- **Bleu de Bresse** :
  Bleu de Bresse
- **Block** : Billot
- **Body** : Corps
- **Boiler** : Chaudière
- **Bolt** : Fermeture de culasse
- **Bolt handle** : Levier d'éjection
- **Bond** : Obligation
- **Boning knife** :
  Couteau à désosser
- **Bonnet** : Coiffe
- **Boot** : Botte
- **Borderline** : Borderline
- **Bore** : Galère
- **Bottle of beer** :
  Canette de bière
- **Bow** : Nœud
- **Bow** : Archet

- **Bow tie** : Nœud papillon
- **Bowl** : Bol
- **Bowls** : Boules
- **Box** : Boîtier
- **Box** : Loge
- **Box spring** : Sommier
- **Bra** : Soutien-gorge
- **Braces** : Bretelles
- **Brain** : Cerveau
- **Breast** : Poitrine
- **Breast pocket** :
  Poche poitrine
- **Breathlyser** : Alcootest
- **Breech** : Culasse
- **Bribe** : Pot-de-vin
- **Bridge** : Chevalet
- **Bridge table** :
  Table de bridge
- **Brisket** : Bréchet
- **Brother-in-law** : Beau-frère
- **Buffet** : Commode
- **Bulb of heel** : Bulbe du talon
- **Bumper** : Butoir
- **Bunch of flowers** :
  Bouquet de fleurs
- **Bunk** : Couchette
- **Buoy** : Bouée
- **Busby** : Ourson
- **Butler** : Maître d'hôtel
- **Button** : Bouton
- **Buttonhole** : Boutonnière
- **Buying the gifts** :
  l'Achat des cadeaux

- **Cabinet** : Enceinte
- **Calcaneus** : Malléole
- **Calf** : Mollet
- **Camembert** : Camembert
- **Can of French beans** :
  Boîte de haricots verts
- **Can opener** : Ouvre-boîte
- **Canadian crutch** :
  Béquille canadienne
- **Candelabra** : Chandelier
- **Canned tomatoes** :
  Boîte de tomates
- **Cannister** :
  Capot de bout d'arbre
- **Canopy** : Verrière

- **Cap** : Casquette
- **Cap** : Chapeau
- **Car** : Voiture
- **Car** : Caisse
- **Caravan** : Caravane
- **Cards** : Cartes
- **Carpus** : Carpe
- **Cashier** : Caissier
- **Cashier** : Caissière
- **Cash register** : Caisse
- **Cast iron casing** :
  Corps en fonte
- **Catch** : Cuiller
- **Catfish** : Poisson-chat
- **Centre drawer** : Tiroir central
- **Chandelier** : Lustre
- **Chapter** : Chapitre
- **Chastity** : Chasteté
- **Chasuble** : Chasuble
- **Chef's hat** : Toque de chef
- **Cheque** : Chèque
- **Chest** : Poitrine
- **Child from first marriage** :
  Enfant du 1er lit
- **Child from second marriage** :
  Enfant du 2e lit
- **Chinchilla** : Chinchilla
- **Chin** : Menton
- **Chrysanthemum** :
  Chrysanthème
- **Chuck short rib** :
  Haut de côtes
- **Cigarette** : Cigarette
- **Cirrostratus** : Cirro-stratus
- **Claw** : Griffe
- **Climbing** : Montée
- **Clinches** : Rivets
- **Cloister** : Cloître
- **Clothes pin** : Pince à linge
- **Coat hanger** : Cintre
- **Cockroach** : Blatte
- **Collar** : Col
- **Collar** : Collier
- **Collar bone** : Clavicule
- **Collection box** : Tronc
- **Comb** : Crête
- **Combat boots** : Rangers
- **Come a cropper (to)** :
  Prendre une veste
- **Common rafter** : Chevron

- **Compass** : Boussole
- **Complement** : Complément
- **Computer** : Ordinateur
- **Comté** : Comté
- **Concentration camp** :
  Camp de concentration
- **Conclave** : Conclave
- **Condom** : Préservatif
- **Conductor** : Chef d'orchestre
- **Conger eel** : Congre
- **Conning tower** : Kiosque
- **Consonant** : Consonne
- **Constituency** :
  Circonscription
- **Contact points** :
  Vis platinées
- **Controls** : Réglages
- **Convent** : Couvent
- **Cope** : Chape
- **Corkscrew** : Tire-bouchon
- **Cornice** : Corniche
- **Coronary band** : Bourrelet
- **Corpse** : Cadavre
- **Corruption** : Corruption
- **Counter** : Guichet
- **Couscous pot** : Couscoussier
- **Cove** : Crique
- **Cover** : Couvercle
- **Crater** : Cratère
- **Credit** : Crédit
- **Credit card** : Carte de crédit
- **Creator** : Créateur
- **Creditor** : Créancier
- **Creep** : Enflure
- **Creep** : Erreur humaine
- **Crest** : Crête
- **Crocodile** : Crocodile
- **Crosier** : Crosse
- **Cross-bar** : Traverse
- **Crown** : Couronne
- **Cuff** : Poignet
- **Cumulonimbus** :
  Cumulo-nimbus
- **Curate** : Vicaire
- **Curtain** : Rideau
- **Curtain rail** :
  Tringle à rideaux
- **Cushion** : Coussin
- **Customer** : Consommateur

- **Dab** : Limande
- **Dachshund** : Teckel
- **Daughter-in-law** :
  Belle-fille
- **Debtor** : Débiteur
- **Decanter** : Carafe
- **Deceased** : Défunt
- **Decoration** : Décoration
- **Deer crossing** :
  Passage d'animaux savages
- **Defence speech** : Plaidoirie
- **Demagogy** : Démagogie
- **Demi-semiquaver** :
  Triple croche
- **Demob** : Quille
- **Desk** : Bureau
- **Detachable collar** :
  Collerette amovible
- **Devil** : Diable
- **Devotion** : Dévotion
- **Diocese** : Diocèse
- **Discount** : Escompte
- **Diva** : Diva
- **Divine** : Divin
- **Dock** : Tronçon
- **Dog blocks** : Griffes
- **Dogholes** : Trous pour valet
- **Door panels** : Sliding doors
- **Dove** : Colombe
- **Down** : Duvet
- **Drawbridge** : Pont-levis
- **Dress** : Robe
- **Dressed** : Sapé
- **Drive** : Pulsion
- **Dromedary** : Dromadaire
- **Duck** : Canard
- **Dune** : Dune
- **Duty free shop** :
  Boutique hors taxe

- **Ear, nose and throat
  specialist** :
  Oto-rhino-laryngologiste
- **Earlobe** : Lobe de l'oreille
- **Earthquake** :
  Tremblement de terre
- **Eclipse** : Éclipse
- **Ecologist** : Écologiste
- **Ecstasy** : Extase

- **Electric chair** :
  Chaise électrique
- **Electric guitar** :
  Guitare électrique
- **Electric heater** :
  Chauffage électrique
- **Electric post** :
  Poteau électrique
- **Electric shaver** :
  Rasoir électrique
- **Electric torch** :
  Lampe de poche
- **Emergency brake** :
  Signal d'alarme
- **Emmenthal** : Emmenthal
- **Emperor** : Empereur
- **Encyclical** : Encyclique
- **Engine room** :
  Chambre des machines
- **Entrance ramp** :
  Bretelle d'accès
- **Epitaph** : Épitaphe
- **Epithet** : Épithète
- **Escalator** : Escalier mécanique
- **Escape** : Évasion
- **Eternal** : Éternel
- **Exhaust nozzle** : Tuyère
- **Exit ramp** : Bretelle de sortie
- **Eyeball** : Globe oculaire
- **Eyebrow** : Sourcil
- **Eyelashes** : Cils
- **Eyelid** : Paupière
- **Eye stay** : Patte d'œillets

- **Faith** : Foi
- **Family portrait** :
  Portrait de famille
- **Fantasy** : Fantasme
- **Fatigue dress** : Treillis
- **Female adviser** : Égerie
- **Femur** : Fémur
- **Fibula** : Péroné
- **File** : Lime
- **Fine** : Contravention
- **Fire-dogs** : Chenets
- **Firefly** : Luciole
- **Flag** : Fanion
- **Flank** : Flanc
- **Flap** : Rabat

- **Flap** : Volet de courbure
- **Flap hydraulic jack** :
  Vérin de commande de volet
- **Flat** : Bémol
- **Flexible hose** : Flexible
- **Floor glide** : Patin
- **Flush handle** :
  Manette de chasse
- **Flying buttress** :
  Arc-boutant
- **Flying instruments** :
  Instruments de vol
- **Foam** : Écume
- **Fog** : Brouillard
- **Forearm crutch** :
  Béquille d'avant-bras
- **Forehead** : Front
- **Four-poster bed** :
  Lit à baldaquin
- **Fracture** : Fracture
- **Fraudulent** : Frauduleux
- **Frets** : Barrettes
- **Fried rice** : Riz cantonais
- **Front placket** :
  Gorge de chemise
- **Front sight** : Guidon
- **Frozen boiled spinach** :
  Épinards en branches surgelés
- **Frozen prawns** :
  Crevettes surgelées
- **Frozen snails** :
  Escargots surgelés
- **Funeral** : Obsèques
- **Fuse** : Détonateur de retard

- **Galaxy** : Galaxie
- **Gangrene** : Gangrène
- **Garter belt** : Porte-jarretelles
- **Genitalia** : Organes génitaux
- **Get a tan (to)** : Bronzer
- **Gift** : Cadeau
- **Gills** : Branchies
- **Ginger** : Gingembre
- **Glass** : Verre
- **Glass of red wine** :
  Ballon de rouge
- **Glasses** : Lunettes
- **Glossary** : Glossaire
- **Gold** : Or

- **Gold plate** : Plaqué or
- **Golf tee** : Tee de golf
- **Gore area** : Divergent
- **Gournay** : Gournay
- **Graduated scale** :
  Échelle des temps
- **Grandfather** : Grand-père
- **Great-grandmother** :
  Arrière-grand-mère
- **Great anteater** : Tamanoir
- **Grog** : Grog
- **Grotto** : Grotte
- **Ground to air missile** :
  Missile sol-air
- **Grouper** : Mérou
- **Guard** : Gardien
- **Gulf** : Golfe
- **Gun** : Revolver
- **Gusset** : Gousset de couplage
- **Gutter** : Égout

- **Hackle** : Piastron
- **Hair** : Cheveux
- **Haircut** : Coupe de cheveux
- **Half note** : Blanche
- **Hand grenade** :
  Grenade à main
- **Handkerchief** : Mouchoir
- **Handle** : Poignée
- **Handle** : Broche de serrage
- **Hanging** : Pendaison
- **Hard-boiled egg** : Œuf dur
- **Hat** : Chapeau
- **Headdress** : Coiffe en dentelle
- **Hearse** : Corbillard
- **Heart** : Cœur
- **Heaven** : Ciel
- **Heavenly** : Céleste
- **Heel** : Cotret
- **Heel** : Talon
- **Heel pakh** : Renfort du talon
- **Helicopter** : Hélicoptère
- **Helix** : Helix
- **Hell** : Enfer
- **Helmet** : Casque
- **Hen** : Poule
- **Herring** : Hareng
- **Hijacking** : Détournement
- **Hind toe** : Pouce

- **Hip** : Hanche
- **Hippopotamus** :
  Hippopotame
- **Holier-than-thou** : Bigot
- **Honda** : Honda
- **Hood** : Capuchon
- **Hook** : Hameçon
- **Hook and eye** : Agrafe
- **Hook disgorger** : Dégorgeoir
- **Hooves** : Sabots
- **Hornet** : Frelon
- **Hostage** : Otage
- **Humanitarian cause** :
  Cause humanitaire
- **Hunting horn** :
  Trompe de chasse

- **Icebox** : Glacière
- **Idol** : Idole
- **Ilium** : Ilion
- **Illegal billposting** :
  Affichage sauvage
- **Immigrant** : immigré
- **In-flight refuelling probe** :
  Perche de ravitaillement
- **Infallibility** : Infaillibilité
- **Infected blood** :
  Sang contaminé
- **Inheritance** : Héritage
- **Injustice** : Injustice
- **Inlet** : Bras de mer
- **Innocent** : Innocent
- **Insemination** : Insémination
- **Intestine** : Intestin
- **Invitations** : Invitations
- **Island** : Terre-plein central

- **Jellyfish** : Méduse
- **Jerk** : Tronche de cake
- **Jet engine** : Réacteur
- **Jet lag** : Décalage horaire
- **Joint** : Pétard
- **Keffyeh** : Keffieh
- **Key** : Curseur
- **Key** : Cheville mécanique
- **Keystone** : Clef de voûte
- **Kilt pin** : Épingle de kilt
- **King post** : Poinçon

- **Kite** : Cerf-volant
- **Knee** : Genou
- **Knee cap** : Rotule
- **Knitting** : Tricot

- **Labrador** : Labrador
- **Lace** : Dentelle
- **Lamprey** : Lamproie
- **Lampshade** : Abat-jour
- **Lane** : Voie de circulation
- **Launch** : Chaloupe
- **Lawyer** : Avocat
- **Leader board** :
  Planche à vent
- **Leech** : Sangsue
- **Left bank** : Rive gauche
- **Left pedestre** :
  Caisson gauche
- **Leg** : Pied
- **Leg brace** : Entretoise
- **Leg of lamb** : Gigot
- **Leg of mutton handle** :
  Manche à gigot
- **Letter of credit** : Traite
- **Levier** : Branche
- **Lip** : Lèvre
- **Liquid rocket booster** :
  Fusée à propergol liquide
- **Literary prize** : Prix littéraire
- **Live-in lover** : Concubin
  notoire
- **Lobe** : Lobe
- **Lock** : Serrure
- **Loden** : Loden
- **Log** : Bûche
- **Loin** : Carré
- **Loop ramp** :
  Bretelle de raccordement
- **Lord** : Seigneur
- **Lorgnette** : Face-à-main
- **Lottery** : Loterie
- **Louse** : Pou
- **Low bow** : Courbette
- **Lox tank baffler** :
  Réflecteur de réservoir
  d'origine liquide
- **Lug** : Ergot
- **Luxury** : Luxe

- **Mach and speed indicator** :
  Anémomachmètre
- **Magazine release** :
  Levier d'ouverture du magasin
- **Magnifier** : Loupe
- **Maid** : Bonne
- **Mandarin cap** :
  Chapeau de mandarin
- **Manure heap** :
  Tas de fumier
- **Mattress** : Matelas
- **Mattress cover** : Alèse
- **Mayfly** : Éphémère
- **Media** : Médias
- **Meditation** : Meditation
- **Menu** : Menu
- **Mesosphere** : Mésosphère
- **Metatarsal** : Metatarse
- **Metronome** : Métronome
- **Midsole wedge** : Biseau
- **Milk** : Lait
- **Milking** : Traite
- **Mimolette** : Mimolette
- **Mince** : Hachis
- **Mink** : Vison
- **Minor road** :
  Route secondaire
- **Mirador** : Mirador
- **Mirror** : Glace
- **Missile** : Missile
- **Missile launch rail** :
  Rail de lancement de missiles
- **Missile tube** :
  Tube lance-missiles
- **Mistress** : Maîtresse
- **Miter** : Mitre
- **Mitt** : Moufle
- **Moistene** : Mouilleur
- **Mongoose** : Mangouste
- **Monk** : Moine
- **Moose** : Orignal
- **Mosque** : Mosquée
- **Mother-in-law** : Belle-mère
- **Motorbike** : Moto
- **Motor unit lever** : Motrice
- **Motorway** : Autoroute
- **Mousetrap** : Piège à souris
- **Moustache** : Moustache
- **Mouth** : Bouche
- **Mule** : Mule

- **Multiple sclerosis** :
  Sclérose en plaques
- **Music stand** : Pupitre
- **Muzzle** : Museau

- **Nail cleaner** : Cure-ongles
- **Nail nick** : Onglet
- **Nail polish** : Vernis à ongles
- **Narcissistic** : Narcissique
- **Nave** : Nef
- **Navel** : Nombril
- **Nebula** : Nébuleuse
- **Neck** : Collet
- **Neck** : Manche
- **Neck** : Tête
- **Necklace** : Collier
- **Nemès** : Nemès
- **Neurotic** : Névrotique
- **Nipple** : Mamelon
- **Nostril** : Narine
- **Nostril** : Naseau
- **Note** : Note
- **Novice** : Novice
- **Nuclear bomb** :
  Bombe atomique
- **Nuclear power reactor** :
  Surgénérateur
- **Nuncio** : Nonce
- **Nurse** : Infirmière

- **Oak** : Chêne
- **Observatory** : Observatoire
- **Œdipus** : Œdipe
- **Œsophagus** : Œsophage
- **On-off button** :
  Commande marche/arrêt
- **Open rear sight** :
  Hausse réglable
- **Orbit** : Orbite
- **Outsole** : Semelle extérieure
- **Ovary** : Ovaire
- **Overflow** : Trop-plein
- **Overshoe** : Couvre-chaussure
- **Oyster** : Huître

- **Pacemaker** :
  Stimulateur cardiaque

- **Padding** : Rembourrage
- **Painting** : Tableau
- **Paper clip** : Trombone
- **Parliamentary immunity** :
  Immunité parlementaire
- **Parlour** : Parloir
- **Party financing** :
  Financement des partis
- **Pass away (to)** : Trépasser
- **Pastern** : Paturon
- **Peak** : Faîte
- **Peak** : Visière
- **Pebble** : Galet
- **Peeler** : Couteau à éplucher
- **Peking duck** : Canard laqué
- **Pendulum** : Balancier
- **Penis** : Pénis
- **Perfecto** : Perfecto
- **Periople** : Muraille
- **Petit suisse** : Petit-suisse
- **Phallic** : Phallique
- **Phobic** : Phobique
- **Pile** : Magot
- **Pilot light** : Voyant lumineux
- **Pinball** : Billard électrique
- **Pineapple can** :
  Boîte d'ananas
- **Pitcher** : Pichet
- **Pitchfork** : Fourche
- **Pivot** : Axe de balancier
- **Plane crash** :
  Catastrophe aérienne
- **Plane ticket** : Billet d'avion
- **Plant** : Plante verte
- **Plastic bag** : Sac plastique
- **Platform** : Quai
- **Pleonasm** : Pléonasme
- **Plinth** : Plinthe
- **Plural** : Pluriel
- **Pole position** : Pole position
- **Polecat** : Putois
- **Pont l'évêque** : Pont-l'évêque
- **Port** : Bâbord
- **Port sail plane** :
  Gouvernail de plongée avant
- **Portable shower head** :
  Douchette
- **Portrait** : Portrait
- **Pot of Jam** :
  Pot de confitures

- **Power** : Pouvoir
- **Prawn** : Crevette
- **Primer** : Amorce
- **Principal rafter** : Arbalétrier
- **Prison** : Violon
- **Problem** : Lézard
- **Procession** : Procession
- **Projection** : Projection
- **Propeller** : Hélice
- **Prostate** : Prostate
- **Pruning shears** : Sécateur
- **Pull ring** : Anneau
- **Pumps** : Escarpins
- **Puncture** : Crevaison
- **Pupil** : Pupille
- **Pylon** : Pylône

- **Quarter** : Quartier

- **Race** : Race
- **Rack** : Carré de côtelettes
- **Rainbow** : Arc-en-ciel
- **Raincoat** : Imperméable
- **Rape** : Viol
- **Rare** : Saignant
- **Raw fish** : Poisson cru
- **Reactor** : Réacteur
- **Real pain** : Prise de tête
- **Rear view mirror** :
  Rétroviseur
- **Rear wind** : Vent arrière
- **Record pad** :
  Plaque de couche antérieure
- **Recovery** : Guérison
- **Red carpet** : Tapis rouge
- **Reed** : Anche
- **Reef knot** : Nœud plat
- **Refrigerate (to)** :
  Réfrigérer
- **Regression** : Régression
- **Rest area** : Aire de repos
- **Retum section** :
  Retour de bureau
- **Reverser** : Inverseur
- **Rib cage** : Cage thoracique
- **Ricefield** : Rizière
- **Rifle** : Carabine
- **Rolling** : Roulis

- **Rolling pin** :
  Rouleau à pâtisserie
- **Roof** : Toit
- **Rump** : Selle
- **Running shoe** :
  Chaussure de course à pied

- **Sacrum** : Sacrum
- **Safe** : Coffre-fort
- **Safety button** :
  Poussoir de sûreté
- **Satety pin** : Goupille
- **Sail bars** : Lattis
- **Saint marcellin** :
  Saint-marcellin
- **Sainte maure** : Sainte-maure
- **Saucers** : Soucoupes
- **Savings** : Épargne
- **Scallop** :
  Coquille Saint-Jacques
- **Scarf** : Foulard
- **Scenery** : Décor
- **Schizophrenia** :
  Schizophrénie
- **Scissors** : Ciseaux
- **Scrabble** : Scrabble
- **Screech owl** : Chat-huant
- **Screwdriver** : Tournevis
- **Seat** : Siège
- **Sea gull** : Mouette
- **Sea spray** : Embruns
- **Secret funds** : Caisse noire
- **Secretary** : Secrétaire
- **Senior citizen's rail pass** :
  Carte du réduction
- **Serving apron** :
  Tablier de service
- **Shackle** : Anneau
- **Shame** : La honte
- **Shank** : Jarret
- **Share** : Action
- **Sharpening steel** : Fusil
- **Sheep** : Mouton
- **Sheet** : Drap
- **Shirt** : Chemise
- **Shirt tail** : Pan de chemise
- **Shoe laces** : Lacets
- **Shoe tree** : Embauchoir
- **Shorts** : Short

- **Shoulder** :
  Bande d'arrêt d'urgence
- **Shoulder** :Épaule
- **Shoulder blade :**Omoplate
- **Shuttlecock** : Volant
- **Sickles** : Plumes arquées
- **Side handrail** :
  Barre de maintien
- **Side walls** :
  Mamelle latérale
- **Signet ring** : Chevalière
- **Silurid** : Silure
- **Singular** : Singulier
- **Sinister** : Patibulaire
- **Sirloin** : Contre-filet
- **Skilift** : Remonte-pente
- **Skimmer** : Écumoire
- **Skirt** : Jupe
- **Ski school** : École de ski
- **Skull** : Crâne
- **Slanting eyes** : Yeux bridés
- **Sleeper** : Traverse
- **Sleeve** : Manche
- **Sleeve placket** : Patte
- **Slip** : Combinaison
- **Snow** : Neige
- **Snowshoe** : Raquette
- **Soap dish** : Porte-savon
- **Soccer field** :
  Terrain de football
- **Sole** : Semelle
- **Sole meuniere** :
  Sole meunière
- **Son-in-law** : Gendre
- **Sorrow** : Chagrin
- **Soup** : Soupe
- **Space shuttle** :
  Navette spatiale
- **Speaker** : Haut-parleur
- **Spear blade** : Grande lame
- **Speculate (to)** : Spéculer
- **Speculation** : Spéculation
- **Speculum** : Spéculum
- **Spell (to)** : Épeler
- **Sperm whale** : Cachalot
- **Spindle locking plate** :
  Plaque d'arrêt de la vis sans
  fin
- **Spire** : Flèche
- **Spring** : Ressort
- **Spring roll** :
  Rouleau de printemps
- **Spring slot** :
  Encoche de ressort
- **Spur** : Éperon
- **Spur** : Ergot
- **Stabilizer** : Stabilisateur
- **Starboard diving plane** :
  Barre de plongée
- **Steam** : Vapeur
- **Sternum** : Sternum
- **Stew** : Civet
- **Stirrup** : Étrier
- **Stock** : Bord d'attaque
- **Stock** : Crosse
- **Stock Exchange** : Bourse
- **Stole** : Étole
- **Stomach** : Estomac
- **Stork** : Cigogne
- **Storm** : Tempête
- **Stoup** : Bénitier
- **Stout** : Corpulent
- **Straight skirt** : Jupe droite
- **Stretcher-bearer** :
  Brancardier
- **Strings** : Cordes
- **Striped shirt** : Chemise rayée
- **Strut** : Contrefiche
- **Sturgeon** : Esturgeon
- **Suicide** : Suicide
- **Sun** : Soleil
- **Superior vena cava** :
  Veine cave supérieure
- **Supposed father** :
  Père présumé
- **Surplice** : Surplis
- **Survivor** : Survivant
- **Suspended sentence** :
  Sursis
- **Swagger bag** : Sac bavolet
- **Swastika** : Croix gammée
- **Swiss knife :** Couteau suisse
- **Switch** : Aiguillage
- **Swivel hook** :
  Crochet pivotant
- **Swivel pin** :
  Anneau grenadière
- **Synod** : Concile
- **Syringe** : Seringue

- **Tablet** : Cachet
- **Tadpole** : Têtard
- **Takeoff** : Décollage
- **Tambourine** : Tambourin
- **Tapir** : Tapir
- **Tarsus** : Tarse
- **Tartan blanket** :
  Couverture écossaise
- **Tasting cup** : Taste-vin
- **Tea** : Thé
- **Teddy bear** :
  Ours en peluche
- **Television** : Télévision
- **Temple** : Temple
- **Tepee** : Tipi
- **Test tube baby** :
  Fécondation in vitro
- **Thigh** : Cuisse
- **Tie beam** : Entrait
- **Toe** : Orteil
- **Toe** : Rive externe
- **Toe box** : Bout
- **Toe clip** : Pince
- **Toes** : Doigts
- **Toilet bowl** : Cuvette
- **Toilet paper** : Papier toilette
- **Tombstone** : Pierre tombale
- **Tongue** : Languette
- **Tongue depressor** :
  Abaisse-langue
- **Too much** : Trop
- **Tool drawer** : Tiroir à outils
- **Tool well** : Auge à outils
- **Toothpick** : Cure-dent
- **Top** : Plateau
- **Torpedo** : Torpille
- **Tower** : Tour
- **Track** : Voie
- **Traffic lights** :
  Feux de signalisation
- **Tragus** : Tragus
- **Train** : Rame
- **Tremolo arm** :
  Bras de vibrato
- **Triple bars** : Barres de spa
- **Tripod cane** : Canne tripode
- **Truffle** : Truffe
- **Truncheon** : Matraque
- **Tumbler holder** :
  Porte-verre

- **Tuning fork** : Diapason
- **Turbine compressor shaft** :
  Arbre turbine compresseur
- **Tureen** : Soupière
- **Turkish toilets** :
  Cabinets à la turque
- **Turn one's coat (to)** :
  Retourner sa veste
- **Turnback** :
  Retour de protection
- **Turnstile** : Tourniquet
- **Tweezers** : Pince à épiler
- **Typewriter** : Machine à écrire

- **U-bend** : Siphon
- **Ulna** : Cubitus
- **Underarm crutch** :
  Béquille commune
- **Underground station** :
  Station de métro
- **Unfortunate mistake** :
  Bavure
- **Uppers** : Empeigne

- **Valencay** : Valençay
- **Varicose** : Variqueux
- **Vault** : Caveau
- **Verb** : Verbe
- **Video supervision** :
  Surveillance vidéo
- **Vomit (to)** : Vomir
- **Vow** : Vœu
- **Vowel** : Voyelle

- **Wall** : Mur
- **Wander around (to)** : Zoner
- **War bonnet** :
  Parure de guerre
- **Warding** :
  Découpage électoral
- **Wart** : Verrue
- **Washbasin** : Lavabo
- **Washing up liquid** :
  Liquide à vaisselle
- **Wattle** : Fanon
- **Weightlessness** :
  Apesanteur

- **Wheelchair** :
  Fauteuil roulant
- **Wide-brimmed hat** :
  Capeline
- **Windmill** : Moulin à vent
- **Windshaft** : Arbre
- **Windshield** : Pare-brise
- **Wing box** : Caisson de voilure
- **Wings** : Coulisses
- **Winkle** : Bigorneau
- **Wiretapping** :
  Écoute telephonique
- **Withers** : Garrot
- **Wok** : Wok
- **Women's magazine** :
  Magazine féminin
- **Wood saw** : Scie à bois
- **Word** : Mot
- **Work surface** :
  Plan de travail
- **Workbench** : Établi
- **Wrack** : Goémon
- **Wreath** : Couronne
- **Wreck** : Épave
- **Wrist** : Poignet
- **Writing slide** : Tirette

- **X-ray** : Radiographie

- **Yacht** : Yacht
- **Yamaha** : Yamaha
- **Yarmulke** : Calotte
- **Yellow** : Jaune

- **Zenith** : Zenith

Please contact our Sales Department for a
FREE catalogue, containing information on
other titles published by

MICHAEL O'MARA BOOKS LIMITED
9 Lion Yard
Tremadoc Road
London SW4 7NQ
Tel: 0171-720-8643
Fax: 0171-627-8953